More Conversations with
Remarkable Women

2007 Commemorative Edition

Williamsburg, Virginia

_____

Interviews by Joy Brady
Word Pictures by Sandy Lenthall
Photographs by Cary Oliva and Dr. Ellen Rudolph

Cover photo by Cary Oliva
Cover designs by Dr. Ellen Rudolph
Interior design by Karin Clamann

Copyright 2003, 2007

ISBN 978-0-6151-3694-3

Published by Sanjoy Publishing
Williamsburg, Virginia

Printed in the United States of America

Forward

The stories of the women included in this book represent individual efforts within a slice of time. These Williamsburg women are prototypes of women throughout the country at a certain time and place in our history. The interviews point out, also, that everyone has a story to tell.

The native peoples of this area followed the traditions of many early groups by teaching their younger members traditions, values, spiritual matters of importance and wisdom of the "tribe" through stories. In each of the interviews in this book, the women were asked to speak to the young women of today which gives us a record of some thoughts considered to be important by some women of the present. These women have accomplished something in their lives *"worthy of being or likely to be noticed"* (The Merriam-Webster Dictionary) and what might be held valuable for passing on to the next generation of women.

As the mayor of a city, involved in the commemoration of our beginnings 400 years ago, I see how significant women have been in our city's history, in our development and that we, as a community, are the blending of many people, many stories. Keeping a record of these people provides an archival treasure.

This book is a meaningful and significant tribute to another remarkable woman, Joy Brady, who enriched this community and all who knew her in countless ways.

Jeanne Zeidler
The Mayor, City of Williamsburg, Virginia

Preface

When the last copies of *Conversations With Remarkable Women* sold, it was clear to Joy and me that a very special experience was ending. The final product gave us great satisfaction. Equally important, we saw the positive reaction of so many people to the book. Feeling affirmed, we decided to close the records and move on.

Then the requests began. Calls came from bookstores and individuals who wanted copies. Would we be reprinting? It was flattering to say the least, so we began to explore a second printing.

At the same time, a parallel idea of doing another book began to appear in our discussions. Maybe we should consider remarkable men? Or should it be remarkable young people? Quite a few people were referring remarkable women to us "just in case you decide to do another book."

It was neither as dramatic as a lightening bolt nor as mysterious as a voice from above, but we began to have a vision and moved into the posture of "working on a second book."

We began our ritual of meeting once a week, setting up appointments and then off we went interviewing, laughing at the car's gps voice giving us directions, sharing ideas and telling stories as well as recording them.

It is difficult to describe the excitement, stimulation, just plain fun that we had and yet always knowing that what we were doing was worthwhile. Somehow, we knew that in this meandering stream of life, we were adding a little recorded history, which might have otherwise been lost or perhaps not unearthed just as other archeological items sometimes remain covered.

Joy's sudden death paralyzed a lot of us. Many gathered to honor her life knowing that they were her "most special friend of all" and realized that this amazing capacity of fully loving and affirming someone was a rare gift which she had given to so many. I certainly was one of those. Losing this "special friend" caused a kind of disorientation and emptiness.

It was too difficult to even think about working on "the book" without her presence.

Our photographer and friend, Ellen Rudolph, suggested that I wait at least six months before giving serious thought to "the book." It was wise counsel indeed for which I'm grateful. As would be expressed in the book of Ecclesiastes, there is a time for waiting, and a time for moving ahead. I could feel the spirit nudging me to begin. With the loving help of Ellen Rudolph, Joy's husband, Donald, encouragement from my husband Ron and Karin Clamann, we made the decision to create an edition which would put together the first publication, the women that Joy and I had interviewed or worked with together, the unique group of remarkable women and, of course, a tribute to our beloved Joy.

With tears because I miss her, with laughter because I remember so much of it with her, with humility because she was one who truly "loved one another" as God instructs and with gratitude to the women who shared their stories with us and helped to make "the book" become a reality, here it is!

Please enjoy,
Sandy Lenthall

Table of Contents

Forward (2003 Edition)

Their names have the ring of fine crystal and the clarity of sunshine. Their lives cast shadows which traverse 400 years in a millesecond. Their memories are like a recurring rainbow, many hued and pregnant with promise...inspiring in the retelling of their stories, calling them back through the Tidewater mists to touch our lives today...Mistress Forrest and her handmaiden Ann Burras, whose adventurous English toes first touched Jamestown sand in 1608...a laughing Pocahontas, who would in time become Lady Rebecca Rolfe, a Virginia lady born. Cicely Jordan, Lady Temperance Flowerdew Yeardley, Mary Johnson, Sarah Harrison Blair, Elizabeth Kingsmill Bacon, Frances Culpeper Stevens Berkeley Ludwell, Ann Hill Carter Lee, Martha Jefferson, Ann Wager, and Lady Skipwith. As we flesh out the bones of these icons, one can almost hear the playful laughter and see the tears of remorse. The stitches of their stories have woven a tapestry of life's patterns. These characters, ladies and others, who stepped out of society's traces to make their own path are each worthy of their own book or chapter...we look through their eyes to see both our past and our future.

Anne Conkling
Local Historian

Celebrating remarkable women, past, present, future,
especially those who allowed us to share their stories in this book,
and also those in our lives whose stories are not found in the pages of this book.

Thoughts to the Reader (2003 Edition)

This would normally be titled "Preface" and "Introduction" but since we haven't done anything according to "Literary Protocol" yet, we decided to begin with a conversation with you.

It all began at Aromas, a local coffee shop, with a conversation about the many women past the age of fifty we had met who were interesting, exciting and had varied life experiences. Perhaps these women are typical of women everywhere. We pondered this and concluded that these women are probably examples of the make-up of most of the communities in America. All these women are from the Williamsburg area, and we quickly discovered the abundance of such women here.

Our contemporary culture doesn't usually call attention to the achievements of women in this age group, so it might be a good idea to collect some of their stories and celebrate the women by putting together a book.

We have different backgrounds and have had broad experiences; however, publishing a book isn't one of them. So it was in 2001 that we began this great adventure having no idea what surprises, pleasures, challenges, learning and mistakes were ahead.

The fun and the laughter we enjoyed as we ploughed our way through never ending piles of paper are hard to describe. The relationships which developed, the inspiration we experienced and the putting it all together possibly outweighs the final product. Except that we do feel good about celebrating in print the stories of these remarkable women and having a record for the next generation as well.

It has been like being on a pilgrimage where we were out to make this journey...but the journey was making us.

We began to frame-in our ideas and with some guidance from more knowledgeable folks began to look for these remarkable women we knew were out there. It was important to include many different kinds of women in all different fields.

Armed with basic questions about if they had mentors, what were the obstacles, what was the most remarkable achievement from their viewpoint and what would they like to tell younger women, we went to their homes with a tape recorder and enthusiasm. Usually, Joy conducted the interviews, edited the material and struggled to put it into some order.

The conversations which you will read are one-sided in that they are in the first person and taken from the taped interviews; however, the questions are implied and woven into the story. It is written in their own words. Thus, there are different patterns of speech, amounts of material covered, emphasis upon different questions, and hopefully a way of expressing thoughts unique to each individual. It is clearly not professional journalism. The conversations turned out to be an overview of their lives and not a complete or detailed biography.

There were two common threads that surfaced among all the women we interviewed. First, they expressed that they did not consider themselves "remarkable" but would be happy to tell us about other women who, in their eyes, were. Second, what they were considered to have accomplished as being remarkable, wasn't. "I just did what I had to do."

The "word pictures" are just that. After the interviews, these were written by Sandy. They are attempts to capture the essence of the woman with a few words instead of a picture done with a brush and paint. They also differ in length and texture because of the individuals.

The photos were all done by Cary Oliva, who is developing her artistic talents in a variety of media. She also tried to capture the individuality of each woman by selective backgrounds, lighting, expressions and postures.

The death of Colette Ringgold, our "cover girl," was the event that made it clear to us that we needed to make another choice rather than continue with the publisher and a planned publication for Spring 2004. It had been our goal to have each one of the women see the finished product. Time waits for no one and after two years of work, we decided to give it our best and "just do what needed to be done."

Enjoy!

Joy and Sandy

Of both the Sky and the Earth. Mary.

Christmas trees and tractors and sheds.
Goats and barns and streams and fish.
CPR and EMT and York River State Park.
Violin lessons, all kinds of music.
Kayaks, bass boats, bicycles.
Curiosity, independence, striving to learn.
Taking risks, working for a goal, confident of herself, grounded.
Of both the Sky and the Earth. Mary.

Seeing her at the farm surrounded by her animals,
One finds a pilot's uniform far from sight.
To see her circled by hundreds of familiar hummingbirds,
One forgets her emergency medical and cardiac training.
To see her cradle her beloved granddaughter,
One misses the cross country bicyclist.
To see her gently stroking the nose of her horse,
One loses the sight of a huge airplane.
She speaks of living two lives.
Of both the Sky and the Earth. Mary.

Mary Apperson

She grew up in an ordinary, middle class family and wanted to fly an airplane. Mary became certified as flight, mechanic and instrument instructor in order to fly commercially and is a wife, grandmother, EMT, an athlete too.

Mary Chilcott Apperson

Born November 20, 1953

My family was pretty typically middle class. Mom, dad, my older brother and sister, myself, and our dog lived in a small Midwestern town. My dad worked for the state unemployment office and my mother was a schoolteacher. I became interested in flying when I was about 17 years old and a friend, who was a private pilot, took me up in a little airplane. At this age, I wasn't sure what I wanted to do. I had wanted to become a veterinarian, but a high school counselor advised me not to pursue that because I was a woman. So, since I was influenced by my airplane experience, I took the money I had for college and got my flight ratings: commercial, instrument, multi-engine, flight instructor's and instrument instructor's licenses. Then I took a job as a flight instructor in Savannah, Georgia where I taught for a year and then moved on to New Kent, Virginia where I taught for 15 years in general aviation.

While in New Kent, I also worked on the planes so I got my mechanic's license. But towards the end I was doing more managerial things, and I really wasn't getting the flying in that I wanted. General aviation is a good job and I enjoyed the people, but there was no security. I did have fun though. I had a friend who also loved flying, and we used to go up and down the eastern seaboard on weekends and stop for lunch somewhere. Other friends had their own planes but they wanted me to fly them. We'd go down to West Palm Beach for a week and other places. But it got to the point where I was in my "30's," and I said, "This isn't going to last very long." It was a lot of fun but it was paycheck to paycheck, you know, no benefits or social security. But I'm glad I had the experience.

A career-turning point was going to an aeronautical college, Emory Riddle University in Georgia. I was working full-time, got married, and taking courses so it took me eight years to get my degree. After working for a commuter airline, I was hired by Delta Airlines as a commercial pilot. This was the best thing for me because I love flying; flying is my job. It's how I make a living, but that's not who I am. My personality is such that, when my husband and I first got married, he would sort of brag about my job and I would ask him not to do that. My job is impressive to most people, but not to me. There are hundreds of thousands of people who do the same thing I do and it's what I do for a living. It's not who I am.

My life is not defined by my job. I live here in Toano on a farm with my family, which is the center of my life. My granddaughter, especially, is the light of my life. I have a lot of interests. I have my horse, some goats and three dogs and I enjoy a lot of outdoor recreation. I love to fish, kayak and bike. The past three years, I've been riding my bicycle with 10,000 other people across the state of Iowa in the oldest organized ride in the country. Also, I volunteer with the James City Rescue Squad and at the York River

State Park. Music is another interest. I'm taking violin lessons and I love it! Family life especially keeps me grounded, and it's what keeps life enjoyable.

My husband and I own the Millfarm Christmas Trees here, so that means replanting seedlings, keeping the grass cut, shearing the trees, then selling them as well as the wreaths we make. This farm has been in my husband's family for 200 years. He's a state forester and years ago I used to fly him all around the area looking for diseased trees. That's how we met. I did not marry until I was 38 years old. Since my parents were divorced, I was a little gun-shy, waiting until the right one came along. And I was very happy by myself. I lived alone for 19 years; I left home when I was 19 and got married at 38. I was very content to be by myself. I would get lonely sometimes but, you know, that's what the phone is for.

I'm at peace here. I don't go for organized religion, but I hope that my spiritual beliefs will influence everything I do, everyday, with the way I treat people and the way things affect me. You can't be in an airplane above the clouds and watch the sunrise or sunset and not thank God for that beauty. I can't walk in the back field, listen to the birds, see a deer or play with my dogs and not thank God for that beauty.

I have always been very independent. I think I was born like this, but I was also affected by seeing my parents live their lives independently of each other. Seeing that let me know at an early age that if I wanted to accomplish anything, I had to rely on myself. From 1993 to 1995, I was on medical leave, and I drove a truck (I got my Commercial Drivers' License) cross-country to deliver cabinets and store fixtures. I needed work, and you do what you have to do.

My advice to young women: "Don't conform to others' expectations for you. Pursue what you love and stick to it! I think of my high school counselor who discouraged me from a profession because I was a female. I should never have listened. Even though I love flying and things worked out, it wasn't right for him to do that. Also, be responsible for yourself. As I said, I learned that from the example that my parents set. They ended up going their own way, and I felt I must always take care of myself."

I'll continue to do what I enjoy. When I have to retire from commercial flying, I have so many interests that I'm not concerned about it. I look forward to new adventures and keeping up with my "old" ones.

Quiet, artistic, this is Betty

In surroundings of gracious comfort, she glances out to her carefully nurtured
Garden area which inspires much of her art work,
Then back to the several paintings she has done in just this one room.
There is a tapestry like painting, a miniature room with a tiny painted chest.
Her artistic expressions are tucked away here, displayed there.

Her dark eyes speak with directness and intensity
As she describes different stages and the discovery of new art forms.
The constant effort is to learn, to find another vehicle of expression.
Beauty with Reverence could be a title for her life's work.
Just as was the book written a few years ago.

The gentle voice hides a determination and perseverance.
To accomplish things "in the right way."
One of St. Paul's teachings* provides a foundation for her work
Many homes in this community include something from her hand.
Art is an integral part of her life. So is humility.
Quiet, artistic, this is Betty.

*Philippians 4:8
"Whatsoever things are true, whatsoever things are honest, whatsoever things
are lovely, think on these things."

Betty Babb

Having a grandmother who taught her to "do it right" in needlework, led to similar goals in painting and gardening. Her paintings and other works of art, large and small, are found in shops and homes throughout Williamsburg and beyond.

Betty Hundley Babb
Born April 16, 1936

I grew up in a traditional, loving family with a mother, father, brother and sister. My grandmother, who lived with us, had a lot of influence on me. I believe I would call her my mentor. She was very talented in music and taught me to play the piano, knit, crochet and embroider. I was knitting squares for the Red Cross when I was five years old. All of these skills are still with me — I enjoy them all. My grandmother also taught me that if you are going to do something, no matter what it is, it's got to be right.

One of my accomplishments was raising three children — that's a big one. They're all interested in gardening in one way or another, but none have started painting. Perhaps the biggest challenge I took on was the 1982 Flower Festival at Bruton Parish Church. Earlier I had read about the flower festivals in England which were held as a way to make money for the restoration or to repair English churches after World War II. Two women even came from England to participate. I also helped work on a book, *Beauty with Reverence*, about the festival. Because of their interest, Colonial Williamsburg (CW) became a participant, and the festival was part of that year's annual Gardening Symposium. This turned out to be a huge project with many, many people involved. That was a bit of an accomplishment, I think.

I was introduced to painting when I was a college student and went to Jackson Hole, Wyoming for the summer. The scenery was so magnificent and many were painting it. It looked like such fun, but it was only after the children were in school that I had a chance to begin some serious painting. As it turns out, I have studied painting locally with Barclay Sheaks now for 24 years. What a help that course has been!

I never dreamed of painting in miniature until, at the suggestion of Sue Rountree, a local miniaturist and author, I attended a school in Maine. It offered classes in a variety of miniature crafts. The first course I took was in faux painting, and I added a seascape to the front of a painted chest. Working so small was a challenge and one that I continue to enjoy. I later took classes in china painting, needlework and quilting.

A definite turning point for me was in coming to Williamsburg in '71 when my husband, whom I must say has been very supportive of what I do, was offered a new position. I was exposed to art classes, flower arranging and gardening, with all kinds of artistic expression. Currently, I send most of my miniature paintings to a dealer in Chicago. Also, I belong to a miniature painting society in Washington, D.C. and enter shows there. Primarily I paint landscapes and still life. I've also illustrated books on CW decorations and worked for a publishing company in New England.

I can't say life gets better as I grow older, but there are definite compensations, grandchildren, for one, and more time to enjoy the wonder in the world around us. I have tried to capture some of that beauty in my paintings, beauty that uplifts and enriches, even if it's just for a few moments. I do believe that we each have talents which are God given and, therefore, should be gratefully shared.

I would advise young people to do the same: "Embrace opportunities. St. Paul said that we should 'keep our minds on what is true, what is just, what is beautiful.' There is so much beauty in this world that uplifts, unlike violence and coarseness." As my grand-mother used to tell me, "Do it right!"

Judy speaks. One listens.

A new painting done by the Inuit, an older painting of Jerusalem.
A wooden sculpture resting on a table. Books stacked everywhere.
Magazines and papers cover the dining room table.
The combination for working and learning and living and enjoying
Makes up the setting in which
Judy speaks. One listens.

Her dark brown eyes catch your attention and continually keep you focused.
Her eyebrows frame and highlight her eyes, moving quickly for emphasis.
Tiny smile lines about the eyes, a few creases about the mouth, all from a face
Which tells her story well.
Her clear, direct manner of speaking could be imagined in a Board Room.
Judy speaks. One listens.

In years past, when few women were economists, she found doors closed.
"Men Only" was often the rule.
There were clubs where she couldn't speak.
She knew that things would change and being part of this was important.
Energy seems to flow in abundance and she has a sense of expectation.
Judy speaks. One listens.

What is it that feeds her mind and nourishes her spirit?
It is theatre in New York, in London, at Phi Beta Kappa Hall that invigorates.
It is books of all kinds which challenge, expand, inform.
It is finding the exact word, reading to a first grader, tutoring English,
Dancing, analyzing data.
It is family. Being wife, mother, grandmother.
Judy speaks. One listens.

Judy Baker

As an only child of immigrant parents, she went to Hunter College and Columbia University in NYC majoring in Economics. Judy worked for the firm of Alan Greenspan, was on the advisory committee to the Secretary of the Treasury during the Carter Administration, and she has had a consultation business in Williamsburg since 1990.

Judy Mackey Rosenblum Baker
Born January 11, 1925

My father loved books, loved discussing things and playing with ideas. Mother had boundless energy and was willing to take a risk. She came to this country alone as a fifteen-year-old because she wanted to study. Both my parents expected me to excel. My parents saved for graduate school because it was expected that I attend. College was not even an issue. When I was asked by friends why I majored in economics instead of science, I explained that I wanted to know ALL about the world in which we live. Economics includes political, social, scientific and international issues. It keeps you alive and thinking.

Columbia University sent me to be interviewed for a job at *Business Week*. I went through four interviews before being asked why Columbia had sent me since they knew women wouldn't be hired. There were no anti-discrimination laws and we were very accepting in those days. I simply went back to the University and asked why I had been sent, only to be told, "Because you were perfect for the job; we hoped you would break the barrier." Later, at the firm which did hire me, I did not get the promotion I had been promised because of the places that women weren't allowed, such as in the private clubs and suites where presentations would need to be made. About this time, I met my old friend Alan Greenspan. I told him my predicament. He asked that I send him some of my current work. I did and he hired me. I became vice president and treasurer of his firm.

Motherhood was demanding of my time and energies. When I had two babies I stopped working. But two weeks later, I called and said that I missed work and was able to work from home, which I did. I developed an economic newsletter and counseling firm. Later (1974), I returned to Alan Greenspan's firm and worked for about twelve years before he went to the Federal Reserve.

I never felt personal obstacles. My family raised me with the thought that I could do anything...it was the world around me that didn't agree. When Alan Greenspan hired me, I was paid less than a man would have been paid to do the job. I wasn't angry in that he gave me opportunities that I would never have had. I knew that this paved the way for younger women. I experienced a lot of "firsts" — first woman in the executive dining room, first woman speaker here and there. I was appointed to an Economic Advisory Board to the Secretary of Commerce during Carter's Administration.

There were many turning points in my life: the decision to go into economics was perhaps the biggest; second, was to return to work after having children; finally, when the Greenspan's firm closed, the decision to come down here and create a consulting business.

Another turning point for me was a result of knowing my cousins, the only Holocaust survivors of my family in Europe. The family experience in Europe made me face the inherent evil in people as well as the good. September 11 shook me. I haven't felt that vulnerable since WWII. We Americans believed that it could never happen here. Now we are vulnerable, like the rest of the world.

Most important are my energy level, joy in living, and living to the fullest possible extent. My grandmother in the Ukraine was like this. She was a risk taker. When it was decided that the Jews had to leave by a certain time, she went to the Governor himself to get permission to stay longer and this was granted to her and her family. I grew up with stories like these.

Another story is about my mother. She was a union organizer in New York in the 1920's. They had a strike for shorter hours and better working conditions. When the boss tried to pull her away from the picket line, she hit him with her pocket book. The policeman who arrested her at the boss's urging told her, "Next time, lady, kick him in the shins where no one can see." At court she told the Judge that it made no sense for this country to have wonderful classes for the new immigrants when their working hours were so long, no one could take them. The judge let her go. Stories — we had lots of them in my family.

To me "older" means more experienced, energetic, and comfortable in who you are, relaxed, but I feel "old" when words don't come as easily.

My advice to young women is what I have told my daughters, " Follow your star. Know what you want and go after it. Never fool yourself; know what it is that makes you happy. Don't lead a life that other people try to tell you, you must be true to yourself. You can fool others but never yourself."

Lately I have become interested in the American Revolutionary period. In fact, I am going to get my information together and write an article debunking Jefferson.

I love volunteering at the Rita Welsh Center. Once a week, I work with first graders at Stonehouse Elementary School working on reading. Also, I love to dance! That's how I met my wonderful husband Russell.

Sister Berenice, A Voice of Love

Tiny, looking almost fragile,
She sits quietly in everyday clothes.
If she was not sitting in a convent, her calling would not be evident.
The first words she spoke introduced us to
Sister Berenice, a voice of love.

As she spoke of early dreams and childhood experiences,
The growing messages became stronger and stronger
Until she faced the question of whom to serve.
In her teens, she made the choice to become
Sister Berenice, a voice of love.

Always the teacher, of both the young and teens.
One can imagine her stooping down to reach the little ones,
To stretch out and be amongst them; to stretch up and relate to the older ones.
There's fun, enthusiasm, wit and warmth in the stories of
Sister Berenice, a voice of love.

She feels close to St.Bede's, her home for years.
Not only students but the poor, the prisoners, the sick and the elderly
Have felt her compassion and assistance.
She lifts her hands out in a warm gesture to the world as she speaks.
Sister Berenice, a voice of love.

Sister Berenice

Growing up in the Depression Era, her mother not only encouraged her in spiritual matters, but worked at a menial job so that her daughter could enter the convent. As a Sister of Mercy, she has taught, ministered to the sick, the poor, the undereducated and continues to do so (following retirement) through St. Bede Roman Catholic Church.

Sister Berenice - Mary Elizabeth Therese Eltz
Born January 7, 1916

My mother was Irish and my father was German. I had an older brother who went off to the seminary to become a priest when I was 12 years old, so I didn't know him until much later. We're good friends now, he's 88, and lives here in Williamsburg. I see him almost everyday.

I'm like my Irish mother, with a good sense of humor, and my brother is more like my father; a German, much more serious. My father owned a small shoe store but lost it during the Depression. He never did much after that. My Aunt Jule played a big part in our lives, for she came to live with us and, for awhile, she was the breadwinner for all five of us. We didn't have a lot. My mother went to Mass everyday to pray for us.

When I was little, my mother would take me, my brother and Aunt Jule to special events at the church on Sunday afternoons. At age five, I wanted to become a priest. But then I would look at the Sisters at the Adoration Service, the Carmelite Sisters, and dream about being a nun. My aunt would read about the "Little Flower," a story about a Carmelite Sister, to my brother and me. The Carmelites live a life of prayer and don't go out. I didn't think I could do that when it was time to make a choice about a convent.

By the time I graduated from high school at 18, I wanted to become a Sister of Mercy. I liked the word "Mercy" and all that it means. My mother encouraged me. She was also my best friend, and she did everything to make sure that I didn't feel obligated to stay at home to help her out. I didn't find out until years later, when I found pay stubs in her drawer, that she had gone to work cleaning offices at night when I was in the convent. She didn't want anything to come in the way of my staying there. My mother was a strong woman.

Becoming a nun wasn't a sudden decision. There were many reasons why I wanted to become a nun, but I think the major turning point occurred when I was a sophomore in high school. There was a Sister Constance who taught Latin. Everyone loved and admired her. There would always be a crowd of adoring young girls in her room after school. I was one of them; I wanted to be just like her. This stayed with me throughout my life. Also, I had thought long and hard about what I wanted to do with my life. I asked a "spiritual director" from my church to help me decide. We met often. After much prayer, I went on a retreat in 1934 and entered the convent. (My father thought I was too young, but he went along with my mother who was delighted.)

There was a boy next door, Bill Fahy, whom I grew up with from grade six on. We even taught each other to dance. We would put records on the victrola and try out all the new steps. One time I asked my brother if he wanted to learn, but he couldn't see why anyone would want to dance. I stayed friends with Bill all through high school, even when he moved away and went to St. Joseph's Prep School. We remained telephone friends; his friendship was important to me. When I made the decision to go into the convent, I told Bill. He accepted my decision...then I didn't hear from him for years. About 15 years ago he called "just to hear my voice." The next year he died.

Convent training was very disciplined, and it is only by the grace of God that I finished. There was visiting from the family once a month, and any gifts that were brought to you had to go to the Sister in charge. There was penance for anything you did wrong, like breaking a dish. I tried so hard to do everything right. To become a Postulant (asking for permission) took six months, then a Novice (wearing a white veil and habit) took two years. This was when we studied for the vows of poverty, chastity and obedience. Then you would make your vows and be able to wear the black veil and habit. I took my final vows in 1937 for life. I certainly had "doubts" off and on, but I never lost faith that this was God's plan for me. My first "obedience" or teaching assignment was in an academy in Philadelphia. I taught everything, including college classes. English literature was my favorite subject, and I especially liked the British authors. In 1951, I came to Walsingham Academy in Williamsburg. Sister Constance was the Mother Superior, my friend and my inspiration from before. I came back to Walsingham three different times.

I told you we had to take three vows when we entered the convent, but there was a fourth vow. That was to give service to the poor, sick and uneducated. After all my teaching years, I retired, but I didn't want to retire from giving. So I went to Trinity College in Washington, D.C. to study pastoral care and social ministry. At age 59, I came to St. Bede in Williamsburg, where I work in the Social Ministry Office and take care of the poor, the sick and the uneducated. God has blessed me with good health, and for that I thank Him.

There is a real problem with the poor and needy, especially young men. The people have problems during the layoff season. The city fathers are not interested in having a homeless shelter here because so many people would come. So Claire McQuade, from St. Bede, wrote a grant, and we were then able to acquire two vans for distributing food. We would go around to all the local grocery stores to collect food, which would be wasted if we didn't collect it.

Looking back on events in my life, I think of how often things worked out for the best. After Vatican II, there were so many changes. Not only were there changes in dress and behavior, but also in the fact that we could make choices on our own. When I made the decision to go into social ministry, for example, I went to work in Levittown, Pennsylvania. This was my two years of "internship."

I didn't drive a car and when I had inquired before accepting the assignment to go there, the Sister whom I was assigned to work with assured me that it wouldn't be a problem. However, once I arrived, she told me that she had made arrangements for me to go to driving school. I wasn't happy about that at the beginning, but I've been glad ever since that I learned how to drive!

Another major turning point in my life was coming to Williamsburg. There was both the teaching and social ministry, and I've had many situations working with the poor and needy. I have liked living in the Mercy community here; I feel at home. God works in your life at different periods in different ways. For example, when my mother was living alone in Philadelphia, most of the family members had died, and I didn't drive a car at that time. Another Sister drove me across to the other side of the city to see my mother every week.

This is my advice to young people: "By living a good life, based on moral principles and dependence upon God, you can make this a better place. Many times you will be swimming against the tide, but the feeling of accomplishment that you have done something worthwhile with your life will be well worth that effort. God asks only three things: to act justly; love tenderly; and walk humbly with your God (Micah)."

Now I'm still helping out at the social ministry office about one day a week, and I go to the Angels of Mercy Clinic in Norge, Virginia, two days a week to help Jeanne and Jeff Black. I also go on hospital visits and take Holy Communion to people in their homes. I've taken on some new responsibilities; I visit a friend who is incarcerated once a week and work with Thumper Newman distributing food at James City Community Church on Mondays, Wednesdays and Fridays from 4-5:15 p.m. (I'm in charge of desserts [Smiles].)

Carolee Silcox Bush

Extra pieces of furniture from the last stage set, pillows piled high
On the couch, a piano which can no longer be played,
Water color paintings, bits and pieces of the many areas and
Organizations benefiting from her volunteer hours.
Carolee welcomes us comfortably knowing that these things are
Not what we've come about.
It is the person, the optimistic, caring, creative
Carolee Silcox Bush that we seek to know.

Her fair complexion and delicately light hair are a contrast to the
Strong, independent, and bright character of this woman.
A teacher, always demanding, caring and lifting students a bit
Higher than they might be aiming, this is a priority.
Performing not only in the classroom, but a life long involvement
With the theater gives deep satisfaction, treasured friendships.

The drive toward education, happiness and spiritual strength
Comes directly from her parents and siblings.
Short on material things, long on love and artistic skills, the
Children in this family grew up enriched, motivated to give.
Stretching out far beyond her family of birth yet still attached to
Her siblings, she extends her compassion to friends as well.
It is Carolee Silcox Bush who shares her story.

Carolee Silcox Bush

Growing up in a large family with little resources and lots of creativity, she began music and drama early. Years of teaching English and involvement with local theatre, Carolee's life has been rich with community involvement and service.

Carolee Silcox Bush
Born December 26, 1934

I was born the day after Christmas. My father wanted to name me something special, so I was named "Carolee," coming from Christmas "Carol," and a family name, "Lee." I was second from the youngest in a family of six children. My family was extremely important to me and is today. My five siblings (one deceased) have always been close, regardless of the fact that we are spread apart geographically. My parents, who never graduated from high school, had high goals for us. One was that all six graduate from high school, which we did. We all had additional education; they pushed the importance of it.

Religion was also an important part of my family life. We belonged to St. Mark's Lutheran Church in Roanoke, Virginia where I was born. Until I was six years old, we had no car so we walked, as a family, one mile to get the bus to go to church. We did this every Sunday. I would say that my parents were devout, not fanatical. My father taught us the church doctrine which we had to memorize for confirmation.

Though I was born on the edge of the Depression, we were able to keep our house because my father always had his printer. We paid just the interest on the house. With one acre of land, we had plenty of food with gardens, a cow, a pig, chickens, and an occasional turkey. There wasn't much money for clothing, so mother sewed our clothes. She used a wash board for cleaning the clothes, and we began saving money for a washing machine. One day a piano became available to buy, and my father asked my mother which she would rather have: "a piano" was her choice.

My mother taught us piano and violin and, since my father had been a professional ballroom dancer, he taught us dancing. The values of education and religion were strong in my life. We had plenty to eat, lots of love and really, I didn't know I was poor. I knew that some children at school had more clothes, more shoes than I did, but I didn't feel poor.

My first mentor was one of my older sisters. At Christmas time, my sister didn't get a doll for Christmas as she asked, so my mother said, "Well, the new baby, Carolee, can be your doll." This sister gave me a lot of attention, was very creative and saw that I auditioned for all the plays and performances possible when I was little. She treated me as someone special and this influenced me throughout my life. I felt very close to her. My oldest sister married when I was six years old; her husband was also a big influence. He saw that I was making good grades in the fourth grade, so he encouraged me to do everything I could to better myself, including encouragement at this young age to think about going to college.

My greatest accomplishment was being able to teach. Teaching is hard, never boring, and I taught high school a total of 34 years. I taught all secondary grades, but the 11th graders were my favorite.

Another accomplishment was the dinner theatre, The Wedgewood. I was teaching in Richmond and became buddies with other teachers. In 1962, five of us decided to start a dinner theatre in Williamsburg. We started saving money and found an abandoned canning factory in Toano ("Charley's Antiques" now). After working night and day, we opened in 1963 and did a variety of productions. The building we originally rented was filled with trash and debris. When my mother came to visit, she told my older sister that she cried all the way home because "Carolee has lost her mind."

The Wedgewood existed until 1971; then I returned to teaching. In 1978, I married a former Wedgewood partner, Charles Bush, who was divorced. I've had a friendship with his wife and a close relationship with his children since they were toddlers. Things fell into place. People's lives are the result of their choices. If there were obstacles, I overcame them by doing what was necessary.

There were important turning points in my life. The first one was leaving a fulltime job and going into creating a theatre. I had doubts about doing that, but I "latched on" to a dream, and I'm glad I did it. Another one was when I went to Hampton University to study black literature. This was at the time of recent integration. I wanted to know more about all my students whom I might teach; studying the literature of a people is a good way to learn their culture. As a teacher, I tried to hold all students to high levels of expectation. We respected each other, and I had a good time with the kids. Then, getting over the death of my close friend, Claudine Carew, whom I helped at a devastating time in her life, was difficult for me.

Presently, my husband and I are in the theatre consulting business (Wedgewood Renaissance Theatre). We do set designs. Last summer we did a project with the Williamsburg Players and dedicated the profits to the Claudine Carew Scholarship Fund.

Coming here to Williamsburg in the spring of '62 turned out to be a good move. I am a happy person, and I don't do things to make myself happy. I do something because there's some worth in doing it. To me being "happy" means taking things in stride and using coping skills.

My advice to young women: "Be assertive about the value of yourself. You are still being too submissive in your relationships with men; for example, some choose to "cowtow" to someone else. Some of you have no confidence in yourselves. As I mentioned before, people's lives are the result of their choices." Also, I'll relate this incident to others because it helped me focus throughout my life on what's important. When I was a senior in college, I was sitting in the coffee shop when three of the important women on campus came in VERY upset, for they were distraught that the doughnuts had not come yet for the reception at the Cotillion, the big dance that evening. This was an epiphany for me and I prayed, "Dear God, may my life not be about doughnuts being delivered on time!"

I'm proud to have been active in the Virginia Education Association (VEA), serving as president of the York Education Association for three years and on the district board of directors for 10 years. Through VEA training I learned a lot and put some of that experience to work in the VEA Political Action Committee for ten years. Currently I serve on the Williamsburg-James City County School Board and was chairperson the year of 2000. This opportunity has allowed me to continue to be a part of the importance of education to people in our community.

What's next? My mother was very artistic and I believe that I inherited some of that ability. I took art classes in college, put it aside until later, and have recently studied watercolor painting. I won first place at the Williamsburg-James City County Fair. I am still involved in my church, St. Stephen's Lutheran, where I sing in the choir. Sometime in the near future I hope to work on a history of the Wedgewood Theatre, a remembrance of my parents and also a piece on my friendship with Claudine Carew. Remarkable? I don't think so. I'm just doing my job.

Elizabeth, a Grand Southern Lady

She is slight and trim, so straight that one wonders if she imagines books
Piled on top of her head as she walks and sits.
Early training in the art of being a lady still shows.
When seated, her hands automatically fold gently in her lap.
Elizabeth, a grand Southern Lady.

In the 1920's, few women went "out to work" in this small town.
She found her interest in history stimulated by the new restoration village.
When the principals were working on this project, she became a "hostess"
Singled out to give special tours.
Elizabeth worked even though she was a Southern Lady.

She ventured even farther for "the foundation" by presenting colonial
History in 18th century costume on a cruise. This was a first.
From her own family, the strength of the church became hers as well.
With catechism learned early, she knows the liturgy by heart.
Elizabeth, a grand Southern Lady.

Her stories of growing up on a plantation sweep one backward in time.
Her concerns about existing problems bring one to today.
Continuing to be active, involved,
She's planning to move with her daughter. A new future.
Elizabeth, is indeed, a grand Southern Lady.

Elizabeth Callis

One of 11 children, her family life also gave her a sound beginning in literature, nature, social graces and religion. Elizabeth taught in public school, then later established Colonial Williamsburg's first training program for the guides and is still learning and teaching.

Elizabeth Pettus Callis

Born February 19, 1906

You will find the Pettus name all the way back to Jamestown in the 1600's when a Pettus was a member of the House of Burgesses. My own family came from Charlotte County in Virginia where we had an old farm dating back to the time when it was called a plantation, Avondale Plantation. In my day and time, there were people, who still worked for us on the farm, who had been from the families of slaves before the war. My early life was very influential in what I have done as an adult. My parents devoted themselves to their children. There were eleven of us; my four brothers were the oldest, then my six sisters, and I was in the middle. My sister Kate, who was four years older than I, was my mentor and best friend. We rode horses together, went off to pick strawberries, did errands for our mother, and were the best of companions. One summer, we went to an outbuilding known as "old John's home" and found this long chest filled to the brim with books. We had a wonderful time pouring over all those books and one in particular was *Bonnie Kate*. I've never seen it since then. Books were very important in our family and we were often given them as presents. I still go to the library frequently to take out books. It's one of those valuable things from my early childhood that has been very important to me, even to this day.

All of the children had chores to do. "If the Lord is good enough to give us berries, we need to do something with them," said my mother, and I remember learning to make jam with my sisters when I was quite young. Mother always had beautiful flower gardens, and the girls would have jobs helping to care for them. This experience combined with my father's "nature walks," where he would gather all of us and take us on trails through the woods and in the meadows while teaching us about the trees and flowers and creatures which we saw. He even taught us the botanical names so that many years later when I was giving a tour at Colonial Williamsburg (CW) to the chairman of a Norwegian university horticultural school, I could talk about our flowers, even though we spoke different languages.

I went on to Halifax County to be a teacher of the first four grades of elementary school. My principal, Mrs. Crawley, was a great influence on me, as she not only was my supervisor at school, but I also lived with her family, as was the custom for single teachers at that time. She was a very outgoing person and encouraged me to speak to groups and take an active role in the community. This is another one of those experiences that helped me out later when I was an escort and gave tours for the Foundation in Williamsburg.

Teachers were required to take additional courses for development, so I went to the College of William and Mary one summer. This was in 1932 and I met my husband who had a business in the town. Two years after marriage, we had a daughter, Ann, whom I'm very happy to be living with in this pretty wooded location. She also enjoys flowers and I go out on the deck almost every day after lunch to enjoy the beautiful natural surroundings, especially Ann's flower beds.

Early in CW's history, I became one of their guides, first as a volunteer, then working part time and finally full time. Probably one of my most important accomplishments was the development of what was their first real training program for their guides. I also taught in the program but continued to take guests on tours, sometimes the "crowned heads of state in Europe." I met quite a few important people, such as Winston Churchill, Prime Minister O'Neill from Ireland, and others. At their invitation, we went to visit the O'Neill's later when traveling in their country. My love of history, which began early and was encouraged by family reading, helped me with school studies. It was continued through teaching and eventually by my work with CW. Having been a part of the community during the years of Dr. Goodwin's time as Rector of Bruton Parish Church, gave me the opportunity to learn from him directly his vision for the restoration. I taught Sunday school when it was in the Wythe House; it seems as though I've always been a teacher.

One of the times which was very meaningful to me, was in the 1940's when CW brought many busloads of servicemen to town for tours. Most of them would then be shipped out for the war. To be teaching them the basic ideas on which our country was founded and for which they were now going to fight was important to me.

Looking back, I have had a long, happy and contented life; it has been a fairly simple one. But I feel that personal manners have often been lost in present times. Being concerned for others and being polite, too, should be just as important today as it was in my time.

I have no special secret or formula for living a long time, except I have walked a lot throughout most of my life. Continuing to be interested in all kinds of things and staying active are definitely things which I believe in. Ann and I have always enjoyed doing many of the same things so that we now go to garden events, to the opera or to visit some of the old homes and admire the antiques. We have always been good friends.

Sue the Collector. Nature and art are her world.

Her home wraps around her like a beautiful shawl. Art is everywhere.
Suntanned, energetic she talks about her love of the out-of-doors.
Surrounded by trees and woods, the subjects are hiking, camping, tennis.
She brightens, shows genuine pleasure when the art in her home is admired.
Sue the collector. Nature and art are her world.
Sharing them is her joy.

Windows high up allow the light and leaves quivering in the wind to be seen.
Cabinets lovingly rehabilitated hold even more artistry.
Metal sculptures in the front yard, a dancing bear on the front hall table;
Every corner is like a picture asking to be photographed or painted.

Born and raised in this area, her roots and nourishment come from here.
The College and the City are the fertile soil in which she was planted.
A Gallery for art, an Occasion once a year, fundraisers for children,
Troubled women are all recipients of her caring, her energy.

Home and family are her focus.
Grateful for opportunities, conscious of an obligation
To contribute, to use what she has to improve life for others.
Volunteer hours spent, countless in number, offered back to the community.
Sue the collector. Nature and art are her world.
Sharing them is her joy.

Sue Donaldson

Growing up in this area, she began as an advocate of the arts and then became a collector. A love of nature increases Sue's enjoyment and support of art as well as many other community projects currently receiving her attention and time.

Sue Sydney Marshall Donaldson
Born July 7, 1937

My first mother-in-law, Jean Sheldon, was my mentor. I was married to her son who was killed in Vietnam. She gave me a different view of life; she taught me to be accepting, loving and caring, and she had the gift of making the person she was with feel as though you were the only one in the world. She was so accepting of me.

When my present husband John and I were married, my in-laws accepted John as a son. We had one daughter and she is Jean's "grandchild" in every way. When she was married we were all there, one happy family. You see, I returned to the Williamsburg area with my young son and daughter for support from my mother-in-law and my father-in-law after my husband was killed. I needed their presence and support. I met my present husband of 35 years through a good friend, and he's now a retired professor from the College of William and Mary.

I am not an artist; I just have the eye for good art. I feel that art needs collectors and promoters, as well as the artists themselves. I became interested in collecting art; my first husband was an artist-of-a-sort and exposed me to art in some ways. Then I went on to learn more on my own.

My involvement with community arts began with "An Occasion for the Arts" in the early 70's. I started out by helping with the food organization and went through the steps up to President of the Board of Directors. Presently, I am still on the Board as Artistic Director. I am the Occasion's "history," the continuity.

This Century Gallery is where a lot of my art comes from. It was important to me to get local artists and craftspersons into the Gallery to give them a chance. I'm still on the Exhibitions Committee. I find that if you do a good job, other challenges come to you. With each experience you gain more insight and proficiency; you grow and mature. I feel I'm a much different person now than I was in my younger years. I'm more confident and a more out-reaching person. (My husband has commented about this, too.) I was the Williamsburg area's representative on the Cultural Art's Commission that gives grants. Also, I was appointed by the county to the committee looking for an area cultural and civic center.

Another strong interest I have is Child Development Resources (CDR), an organization that serves young children with special needs and their families. Its administrator, Corinne Garland, kept right after me to work on their fundraising. I did and it was the hardest job I ever had. For four years I was the Gifts Chairperson for CDR which led to the fifth year when I was in charge of a very successful auction. I was also in fundraising while I was a board member of Avalon, a home for abused women. Each of these challenges took on different dimensions and I learned a great deal. (I'm always anxious to share information with the next person who comes along.)

I haven't had any obstacles, really. I appreciate the fact that I never had to work outside the home and was able to be there to raise our children. I have also been fortunate to be able to give back to the community in which I live. This is important since I have had the time and resources available. There was (and still is) another challenge in my life and that involves adapting to a heart healthy diet. My husband had a heart attack in '95; I learned to cook a totally new way that is less fat for both of us. Since I love cooking and enjoy playing around with new recipes, it wasn't difficult, just challenging.

For my 65th birthday, I gave myself the gift of a white water raft-camping trip down the Colorado River through the Grand Canyon with other members of the family and close friends. We slept out of doors and had a wonderful time. Even with a hip replacement that I had earlier, I'm able to hike. This was a challenge for me and maybe to others as well.

When you begin to age, you have to find substitutes. I can't play tennis now so I do other things. My husband and I are also learning to kayak, and we enjoy camping and bike riding, too. You know, a community nourishes itself. There is a reciprocal relationship when people give and the community gives back. I can't stress that enough to young people today.

Caroline, Gentlewoman of the Fields

Her white solid home sits way back with fields all around.
Since 1936 she's been mistress of this house.
Purchased way back when not quite finished,
They chose this spot to rest and
Caroline became gentlewoman of the fields.

At a time when most women kept the house and the children,
She worked side by side with her husband on
A farming operation new to this county.
She called the brokers, ordered the trucks, kept the house and the books.
Caroline, gentlewoman of the fields.

The next challenge to come her way
After teaching, census work, managing a bus line, giving historical tours,
She went into the town of Toano, to be mistress of the mail.
Meantime, she was also raising a son and had to bury her husband.
Caroline Dozier, gentlewoman of the fields.

Now, she spends much time on the little sun porch out back,
With her dog, "Missy," curled up comfortably on her lap.
The windows allow sunshine and views of the barns, the shed, and the fields.
To surround and warm her. With a wise smile, carefully phrased words
Caroline continues to be the gentlewoman of the fields.

Caroline Dozier

Early in childhood, she had thoughts of teaching. Caroline did that, but she also worked for the Census Bureau, helped to run a bus company, a large farm, raise a son, run a post office and work for the community too.

Caroline White Dozier
Born December 7, 1910

My father grew up on a farm in Fluvanna County, west of Richmond, Virginia by about 65 miles, on the banks of a river that is a little muddy stream that flows into the James River. My paternal grandfather farmed, growing tobacco principally and corn and feed for cattle and, in his middle life, he was voted into the Virginia Senate; he and my grandmother lived in Richmond part of the year and went back to the farm when they weren't in session. One of my father's brothers later went into business in Scottsville on the James River, about 6 miles from the farm, and he became a member of the Virginia Legislature. The James River flooded every several years, when the mountain streams thawed and came down, and it was always an event. I remember playing hooky with a friend from high school and joining in the fun with others rowing around in boats. I had four brothers and one older sister Kathryn, who was 10 months old when I was born. She was like a twin to me. We grew up as twins and acted like twins. She was delayed a year in school, so that we could enter school at the same time. She died at an early age of rheumatic fever that developed during WWI. Then I was the only girl; I missed her a lot.

My father became a station agent and he worked as a beginner in Walkers, Virginia. The object was to pull a station that was a bigger station, paid more and provided better income; so father got a station at Lee Hall in Newport News, Virginia. That's how I got anchored into the lower peninsula; I was born while we lived there. But mother said she didn't think the accommodations were suitable for her baby to be born, so she went to her mother's home in North Carolina. There I was born and stayed until she could travel with me to bring me home. But our family made close and lasting friends at Lee Hall. At the beginning of World War I, my dad's youngest brother served in it. I remember my mother and father, in 1915, going to New York to see him off and to see him back in 1918. Anyway, at the time of the war, we rented a house in Oriano, which is about five or six miles below Lee Hall. But the post office was out on route 60 in Denbigh and that's where I started school.

My grandmother was my mentor. We spent summers with her, me and my older sister, until she died. When we went to visit her, my father put us on the train at Oriano, in the custody of the conductor. She thought I was her pride and joy. She lived to be 84 years old, and I still have a couple of letters that she wrote, and in them, she always prodded me on. She said, 'You know, you can do anything you want to do!' She would recite poetry to me and read stories, things like that when we were together.

Another role model and mentor was Mrs. Madison. She just fascinated me. She was my first grade teacher. Because of her, I went into teaching. She was so interested in everything, and I think that's what drew me to her. She was surrounded with reading material and anything she wanted was at her fingertips. I'd go to the school and sit with her after school hours, and this was even after I was married and living in the Williamsburg area. I had her friendship for a long time; this went on until the day she died. I should also mention that I met Ike, my future husband, in the first grade of school (Denbigh, Virginia). He and another "bad" boy sat behind me, and dipped my curls in an ink well. Mother complained to Mrs. Madison that they were ruining my dresses because the ink stains wouldn't come out. The bad boys were moved across the room. That was my first meeting with Ike.

I was also very influenced by my Uncle Russell, who sent himself to George Washington University and then went to work for the government, rose to become Director of International Mails. I envied him, and I felt then that was what I would like to do, to pursue something in that line because he could take his wife and travel the world over. He would contract with all these foreign nations for the transfer and exchange of international mail. And they would be gone for weeks and months at a time, and then we would visit them some summers.

In 1920, I went to William and Mary to study for teaching. (I wanted to go there because I knew two girls going there from Lee Hall.) There were very few women, and they were mostly day students. There was a World War I barrack building on South Boundary Street. That's where my first quarters were. But my second year there, Uncle Russell in Fairfax County, called me - we had telephones then, and he asked me if I would be prepared to teach school this fall? He told me there was one vacancy in Fairfax that I could have if I was qualified. I went to the Dean who said I would qualify if I went through summer school and took required education courses. I did that, and with my Uncle Russell's help, I got a job teaching grades one through seven in English, writing, and physical education. I taught for four years, always trying to be like my mentor, Mrs. Madison. I was paid $110.00 dollars a month in 1929. I was making my own money, and I was proud of myself.

Also, in 1929, The Department of Commerce in Washington, D.C. put out circulars on every doorpost and mailbox telling people to take the Civil Service exams; we would take their big books that recorded the census and check them over. Then we would take and transform them onto eight and a half by eleven sheets, so they could be machine done, after we were through. The pay was $150.00 dollars a month and that was like gold to almost all of us. I rented an apartment with a friend that I knew in college. You had to go to school for two weeks and learn how to correct what was wrong on the form, and how you modified it, to make it fit into what you were supposed to be doing. I didn't mind the work but it was sort of monotonous. I did have some good clerks 'cause a lot of them were teachers, too. I stayed on until I finished the job.

Ike and I were dating while I was working the government job. For three years, I became involved with his father's Peninsula Bus Line (an interstate one). I gave historical tours for chartered tours along the James River estates. I loved doing that because it was like teaching in another form. In 1930 Ike and I were married and eventually moved to a farm in Toano, Virginia, a place we named "Warrenton." I've been living here ever since. It had lots of farmland for growing crops. I learned what I needed to know with Ike's help, and we planted lots of crops of corn, soybeans, potatoes, cabbage, etc. By 1950, we were well into our operation.

In the growing season, when we had products to sell, Ike would case the fields and report to me. That same day I would need to sell trailer loads of cabbage, or two loads of potatoes the next, etc. My day started at 5 a.m. in order to call buyers in major cities, like New York and Philadelphia. Through telephone conversations, I got to know the individual buyers, and I enjoyed them.

I ordered refrigerated trailers from a man in nearby Suffolk, Virginia. Then we would bring the crops from the field, put them over a belt, package them, and load them into the trailer. When that was done, I prepared the manifest and gave the driver the directions for finding the location of the crop delivery.

By that time I was also an acting postmaster (they called it "postmistress" in those days) of Toano. When the announcement was made in the local press that said the current postmaster was retiring, I went to him and asked him if he thought I could handle the job. I told him I didn't want to give up my business with Ike, but I was sure I could do both. After taking me through the process, he told me I had the job as a permanent postmaster. I ended up putting a big desk in a corner of the post office. I was able to take care of both businesses without having to truck back and forth. I retired in 1986 after working 26 years.

In 1960 Ike died at age 51. I needed help in managing both businesses. The best part of being a postmaster, was the people. I just love people. I knew everybody. Some would say something about me knowing everyone's business. I told them that I didn't have interest in anybody else's business; I was busy with my own life.

As far as giving advice to young people ... I think the hardest thing for young people today has to be deciding what to do. There is so much open to them. Sometimes you just have to reach out and take what comes your way. It will be hard work, like when I had to travel long distances to get my credentials to teach, but I had a sense of gratification. My grandmother said that you don't know anything until you get out and do it - and do it well. Young people need to arrive at that.

Born on the Fourth of July, Betty Dye

White hair brushed back by the wind, she drives the mower down the road.
Horses standing, grazing, dozing in the pasture surrounded by white fences.
The neat brick house holds hundreds of hand painted ceramic pieces, a hand
Carved wooden carousel horse, Christmas miniature train layout, awards and
Ribbons and photos and cats.
A burst of energy, born on the Fourth of July, Betty Dye.

A friend said that anyone our age who had children riding horses was
Probably taught by Betty Dye.
An acquaintance said that she builds fences like a man and paints like a lady.
An employee said that there is no one on earth who is like her and she's real.
A neighbor said she's raised more children than the "old woman in the shoe."
An article said that their old farm was built up by hand and a victim of change.

She talks to animals. A male deer brought his "girl friends" to see her.
Birds flutter about the feeders, land on window sills, sit on the rail fence.
Chickens come running. Guinea hens squawk for food.
"I am what I am." "It is what it is." "Life goes on."
An advocate for children and the land, self assured, open, accepting.
A burst of colorful, life giving activity, born on the Fourth of July, Betty Dye.

Betty Dye

Nourished by extended family in Williamsburg, she was interested in horses when quite young.
Betty was an elementary school teacher, built two horse farms, taught riding, paints porcelain figures,
raised a son, was a surrogate parent to other children and is still on the farm every day working.

Betty Jeanne Holland Dye

Born July 4, 1934

My father was Elton Holland. He was a self-made man who, although he had a formal education only up to the sixth grade, went on in the construction business where he did very well. He was married several times. My whole family lived in Williamsburg. My grandparents had tourist homes on Richmond Road. I went to Matthew Whaley School from kindergarten through 12th grade. (Our class of '53 is getting ready to have our 50th anniversary soon.) I was raised by a "Negro," as people said in those days, and I didn't get to know Mother and Dad well until later. For example, when I had "black measles" my father was watching over me and told me that my mother had tried to abort me. This isn't something that a child should be told.

Where did I get my nourishment and love as a child? I was fortunate in that I had uncles and aunts living all around me on Harrison and Nelson Avenues across from St. Bede Catholic Church, and Mr. Saunders had horses down at the end of the road. My father and mother both rode; my sister Mary Alice always had a horse. I was always the one who got the dolls and dollhouses and hated every one of them. I lived at the barn, cleaning out stalls, had pet chickens, a pet lizard, cats and dogs. I loved all animals but they gave me dolls!

I wasn't lacking for love as my aunts and uncles always made a place for me. I'd go around and see who was having the best dinner and stay there. When my father married Ada, she was really good to us.

After my parents divorced and my mother remarried, my stepfather made sexual advances toward me. When I told my mother, she wouldn't believe me, so I went to live with my grandparents. (My grandfather was on feeding tubes; I helped my grandmother care for him as much as I could.) And then there was a private girl's camp in the heart of the Shenandoah Mountains where my sister and I went. I was nicknamed "Betty Boop" there. We went to camp many years where we had the structure in our lives that was important. We learned so many things, had so many experiences and learned about being responsible. It was wonderful.

One of the things which my mother did well was to make Christmas and birthdays really big. I remember having a room filled with trains and Colonial Williamsburg models and a ten-foot high tree all decorated. She was really active in Bruton Parish Church which is where I was confirmed and married. I'm not into church, myself. Nature is my love and, if there is a God, it is in Nature that I see such a presence.

I went to Madison College, which was an all girls' college then. I hated it. Mother said that I had to go there because of a contract she had made earlier. I left after one year and went to Virginia Tech where I was in the art program and took ceramics, painting, and drawing. They were training art teachers then, and I also worked for the Rexall Drug Company. At this time, teachers had to return to college to take additional courses every five years; I took education courses at William and Mary so that I was eventually certified to teach kindergarden through sixth grades. My first teaching job was in Grafton Bethel School where I had 60 kids; we were located in the library. Those kids taught me a lot that year. It was survival of the fittest. Next was a school in Seaford and finally to Magruder School in York County, Virginia. Unfortunately, the principal (now retired) and I had difficulties, and I believe that may have been why I was assigned to a trailer classroom with 13 boys and all the most difficult children. I developed a system of rewards for good behavior and they became some of my best students. There was an instance when I came to the aid of the principal in decorating a room for a special meeting and the next year, I had a room in the school. In fact, she later brought dogwood trees to the farm.

Page and I have been married a long time. Forty some years, I'm not good with dates. One of the big turning points in my life was moving from Bypass Road out to the Cedar Valley Farm which is the property now occupied by Lowes. You should have seen the farm then; it was nothing. Everything was run down and there was a Civil War era house which we remodeled. We needed everything - a tractor, a lawn mower - like the other one and here I was, a city girl, who learned to drive a car at age 21. So many people helped us because there was so much to do. Carpentry, mowing, building fences, digging a pond ... I learned to do all the work along with the others. Page, my husband, had to work hard to make the payments on this farm while I was teaching full time. We boarded horses for income.

We had a son, David, and I taught him to ride a horse at age six as a help for his problem of dyslexia. I believe that you have to have something in your life that is special. Riding clicked with him. My father was very competitive. I was always competitive and so was David. This caused problems for us at times.

David died of AIDS. Losing him was so hard. He was 38 years old, had had an accident in Florida and was given AIDS infected blood. He came home and lived five years on medication which they had then to extend the life of AIDS patients. I had returned to ceramics some years before, at the nagging of my sister, but it was good because it was something that David and I could do together when he was so sick. He continued working with children and with the 4H group. We only had one family that took their child out of the program because of his disease. I'm still involved with the 4H Program, which I began working with when David was eight years old.

We had built barns, out-buildings and a building which we used as a bunk house where we "raised" four boys who lived out there. "Pookey," my sister's son, came to live with us in 1965 when he and my sister had a problem about his long hair. The boys had to keep the place clean, they had chores, they had responsibilities with the horses, they had to keep school grades to a "C" average, at least, and they learned to work hard. They all have done well and have farms or horses now in their lives in some way.

Turning points certainly include getting the first Cedar Valley Farm. We put 36 years into that farm and taught a lot of children through 4H and horses. We even supplied the horses and trailers for several movies because we could make $100 a day and that helped. We didn't think that we would lose the property because of its historical house, but we did. After selling the property to Lowe's, we bought another farm that we also called "Cedar Valley Farm." It was so hard. I moved a lot of the trees and shrubs and bulbs over to this place.

We've had a lot of help and we're in business again. I've got five wonderful young women working here and we have the 4 H programs, boarding horses and teaching children. I don't have the peacocks but we have guinea hens and "silkies"(chickens).

What I would say to the younger generation is to "stay out of trouble" by getting involved in something that will teach them something and that will help other people, too, like Girl and Boy Scouts, 4H, music, and art. Don't try to be an adult before you are ready for it. I used to tell the parents, "Teach them how to read and keep them on a schedule so they'll feel secure." Television is just awful for children. Lots of the movies are too. Marriage is something that you should know what you're getting into and not be an "easy in, easy out" arrangement.

I've always had difficulties accepting the limitations of my gender. I was never strong enough to do the jobs I'd get into. By accepting some things, which you can't change, like two knee operations so that I don't ride anymore, you just go on.

We're working on this place so that it will tell a story, too. We haven't anyone to leave it all to, but I've set things up so that if something happens to me, the operations with the horses will go on. I have wonderful people working here.

Life goes on. I believe that Nature talks to us and I believe that we need to listen.

Mary, Mary

She sits tall and erect. Her posture is one of assurance.
Flawless, dark skin, eyes that flash and soothe.
She is handsome, she is commanding,
But it is her hands which speak so eloquently for her.
Mary, Mary

Her conversation is like hearing the Old Testament.
She and God are in direct conversation. She listens. He talks.
She talks. He listens. It seems neither contrived nor mystical.
It is simply a dialogue, one to the other.
Mary, Mary

Her stories flow like an unpredictable river.
Not always happy or pleasant. Sometimes of passion and drive.
But always honest and open. Words of struggle, fear, love.
Her hands move in gestures of wonder, then uplifted in praise.
Mary, Mary

Beginning college with seven children, graduating with two more.
Teaching, then more college while her children do the same.
Traveling, feeding the hungry, bringing clothing too.
Her hands carried The Word to China. They clasp in obedience.
Mary, Mary

The episodes are too numerous to tell. Listening overflows.
But the message is always the same.
To study and share the word of God. To feed his people.
Her graceful hands fold in her lap as in prayer.
Mary, Mary

Mary Ellis

Born in Surry County, VA she lived with her parents and eight siblings. Mary married, moved to Williamsburg and had nine children, commuted to Norfolk State College, graduated; went on to Hampton University for a Master's Degree and now operates a food and clothing ministry from her home.

Mary Council Ellis
Born June 6, 1927

I guess I'll start with the fact that my family consisted of my father, mother and eight siblings. I was in the middle of the "pecking order". My mother was a housewife who worked hard, like my father. At times, he was an entrepreneur, other times he was a foreman of a sawmill, and when he did that he had several people who worked for him. The workers knew that if they were in need, my parents would help them if they came around our house. I remember my mother taking a lost parachute and making dresses for children in the community.

My sister Carrie, whom I was the closest to, was nine years older than me and she was perfect. You just didn't see perfect people, but she was. She was the one who told me how to take care of myself, and she was my mentor. She told me what was right and wrong to do, so I really looked up to her.

When she graduated from high school, my father sent her to Virginia Theological Seminary College. Carrie's strong faith led her to want to go to Africa as a missionary, but she never did. She was killed in a car accident coming home from the seminary. It was my mother's birthday, and I'll never forget that. All my hopes and dreams just left me.

When I was ready for college my parents sent me to the same seminary that Carrie went to, but I wanted to go to school at the Agricultural and Technical School in North Carolina. When I went to the school, I had my sister's classmates as instructors. They would tell me that my sister would never do the things that I did. Boy, did I rebel; for example, you couldn't go to church unless you wore stockings; I would deliberately tear mine so I didn't have to go. I would sit on the steps and watch the other students go, and I'd watch them come back. I didn't do my homework either; I flunked out of college to the disappointment of my parents.

I went back home and I ended up getting married at age nineteen. I didn't know how to drive, so I was stuck at home months at a time, having children one right after another. I was overwhelmed.

My faith almost failed me because, even though I was praying to God not to have more babies, I kept having them. I felt worthless and I got to the place where I wanted to commit suicide. But a turning point came. I moved from wanting to kill myself to wanting to kill my husband; I felt he had all the freedom, and I was locked up in the house with all the crying babies.

It was at this point that my life changed: I fell on my knees asking God not to let me do anything foolish. The Lord started opening doors for me; for example, this teacher stayed at our house because she needed a place to stay. I would style her hair at times, and her regular hairdresser liked the way I did it. So her hairdresser took me in and trained me to become a cosmetologist. (Everyone was wearing hats at that time so I also became a milliner.)

Eventually, I went to Norfolk State College and completed my degree. By now I had seven children and a long drive to get to classes. Again, God opened doors when my husband took it upon himself to not only help me get a driver's license, but also find a trusted person to help take care of the children. You know what? I graduated in four-and-a-half years. This was while I had my ninth baby, taking some time off. After graduation I became a teacher, and then went on to Hampton Institute to get my Master's Degree in Elementary Education with a leaning toward special education. After teaching in various schools, I went back to school for social worker certification and then worked in York County for 15 years. I retired at age 65. I've also managed to be ordained, with my son as a Baptist preacher; I'm proud of that.

Reading Jeremiah 29:11, I followed God's plan for me by starting a food pantry with the desire to have a homeless shelter. Praise God, it helps many with families to feed. I'll never forget one Thanksgiving when I asked God for more turkeys to give out. The very next day, someone called asking me if I could use fifty extra turkeys! Another time when the pantry was starting up, I never thought my husband would complete the garage-pantry. I talked to God again, and the next morning my husband said, "This looks like a nice day; I think I'll finish the food pantry." God is faithful. (At this point, we give groceries to 1500 to 1700 people a month.)

My advice to young women is: "Don't give up on your dreams or challenges. Talk to God and also to your good friends. When you can be honest and open, others will be, too. Hopefully, because honesty in yourself causes others to be able to be honest themselves, no one will feel embarrassed or alone. Also, respect yourself and your body since you're responsible for yourself." Finally, I would tell everyone that though I have no idea where what I need is coming from, God finds a way to get it. It's usually on time, too.

Now, I'd like to start a Sunday school....

This is Corinne.

Seeing the big picture for children with special needs and choosing
Excellence as the goal. This is Corinne.

Tall, assured and articulate, she talks about Child Development Resources
With the ease and familiarity that comes from long time association.
To the receptionist, she explains, "If it is family, I am always to be interrupted."
This is having it all, but not "all of the all." This is Corinne.

Strongly anchored by parental values, she achieved what they expected-
Do the best, not just good; educate, give to the community, care about others.
The Jewish faith and her parents' lives were so intertwined that she now lives
Out what they lived and what they believed. This is Corinne.

Quick to smile, expressive and always looking into the future positively.
The agency started in a basement, expanding exponentially.
She makes no apologies for aggressively teaching world wide those
Programs that she has been developing.
This is Corinne.

Daughter, wife, mother, grandmother; roles met with enjoyment and devotion.
Teacher, administrator, promoter, speaker; roles met with growing experience.
Books, the piano, friendships, homemaking; interests which add
Color and enrich her very full life. This is Corinne.

We see that individuals in this large agency matter. She calls by name a little
Child building something taller with blocks... it is not unlike her own story of
Starting simply and adding little by little. This is Corinne.

Corinne Garland

Influenced by her parents, who were influenced by their Jewish faith, she began early in her career directing her energy toward children with special needs. While raising her own family, Corinne developed programs for Child Development Resources which are now used as models worldwide.

Corinne Welt Garland
Born January 1, 1941

My dad was the last of the Horatio Alger stories. He was a middle child. His father died when he was nine, he left school at age 13 to support his mother and siblings and, eventually, became a very successful businessman. He was fired from a job early on and decided that this would never happen again. He would have to have his own business. That's how he ended up owning a lithography company. The importance of education, of excelling in whatever you do, of giving back to the community and service to others shaped my life. That was his life. My mother was the glue for the family. Dad was aggressively busy building his business, but he never missed anything in his daughters' lives. He was always there driving, attending functions, etc. Mother smoothed things over and made everything work. She was a stay-at-home "fifties" mother; therefore, I received a mixed message.

The challenge that was expressed in the poster my father had of a zebra in rainbow colored stripes, "good is the enemy of excellent," was embedded in me. He felt that if you are going to do something, then you need to do it REALLY WELL. My father taught us to do things 110 percent. I remember my parents talking with disdain about other people in the synagogue who weren't doing their part. Philanthropy was important; for example, my father heard a story on television of a child dying and the parents were without funds for burial. He got in his car and drove to the family to give them money for this. My sister also got the "message." She lives a very privileged way of life and runs a program for incarcerated fathers staying connected to their children. My father taught us both, and "the apple doesn't fall far from the tree."

Stella Neiman was my mentor. She was Chairman of the Board of Children Developmental Resources (CDR) in 1972 when I took this job. There is little that I do today in this agency that I didn't learn from her. She taught me about community development, political systems and how to work them. She was a role model for grace under pressure. Not only from an agency standpoint, but it also carried over to her personal life; for example, I watched her as her husband died of cancer and wondered if I could ever be as thoughtful as she was to family and friends during this difficult time. I hope that I could be like her.

When I began with CDR there was a staff of four in the basement of St. Bede Catholic Church and three of the women were volunteers. The dynamic growth of the agency is remarkable; most of what you see here is about people caring about other people's children and the quality of their lives. It has given me such an optimistic world view; the forces of good are all around us. I have been shaped so much by the families I've gotten to know here, and it has reframed how I view what's hard and what's easy in light of the lives of the families who deal with problems all the time. I see mainly the "goodness" of man, for so many donate to the agency who don't even have children in the center. This agency and I have grown up together.

The turning points in my life had a lot to do with my family and my work. When I graduated from high school, my father, who had not finished high school, met with his attorney and his accountant and asked where he should send a smart girl to college. They discussed this and chose Vassar College. This was a good choice because it gave me a different understanding of women, offered me lifelong friendships, and reinforced my parents' belief that "there is nothing that you can't do."

I've known my husband since I was 16 years old. We were married in my junior year of college, and I graduated pregnant with our first child. By having children while I was young, it allowed me to be at home while the children were preschool age. Then I taught in their preschool, and we would all go home and take a nap in the afternoon. When they entered school, I decided to go to work. My profession allowed me to gradually re-enter the work force and continue to parent our children. BUT, there is a tension all the time between working and motherhood. (Now I am looking at another realignment, for my husband is thinking about retirement.)

In 1980 when I had just turned 40, my husband accepted a job in Houston, Texas. He was offered a much higher paying job in Houston, where we lived for two years and were miserable. It took two years to discover that all the money in the world wasn't making this worth what we had given up. We missed friends, Williamsburg activities, etc. At a party when we came back to visit, someone had clipped out an ad for a manager at a naval architecture firm, gave it to my husband and he took the job. We returned. We actually bought back the house we had built and lived in all the years before, and soon afterwards I stepped back into CDR because the director wanted to leave at that time. It is eerie how these things happened, even getting the same home phone number!

I haven't had career obstacles. This agency makes it easy for women to combine motherhood and working. My own life experiences have influenced the work culture here at the agency. I'm very aware of women being at home with family and having a professional life.

I was born in 1941 so the Holocaust experience affected my whole family and their worldview. Being Jewish, they no longer felt as safe and knew that, because of their faith, they were vulnerable. This affected them more than it has our generation. I have felt the exclusion of being a minority group member. I'll give you an example: last night the United Way had a wrap-up of their Day of Caring, with over 700 volunteers. I felt that it was a perfect antidote to 9/11. At the end of the program the blessing that was said did not include me. It is in ways like this that I feel the barriers. Yet I have tried to know the differences between anti-Semitism and thoughtlessness. (We do a lot of work in the agency about dealing with diversity.)

Between my husband and me, we had three grandparents who had come from Eastern Europe. ALL of the cousins disappeared. We don't know how they died, Germans or Russians, but they're gone. Strength comes from my parents, and theirs and mine come from their faith and religion. It really can't be separated. Since my husband and I married when we were young, we have grown up together. Our children were born to us early in our marriage; we have grown up with them as well. So my strength comes from both of my families and children.

I think that the Williamsburg community is unusually supportive of this agency. I am thankful. This is people contributing to something which will improve the lives of other people's children who, eventually, will make the future better. It was a very safe community in which to have a growing family, but I don't think that is so, even here, anymore.

My advice to younger women: "It is possible to have it all but not all of all. Whatever you choose, make peace with yourself about what you have to give up. Being a mother and having a career, you can't be fully one or the other all the time so there are going to be times of tension."

Friendships are really important to me. My Vassar College roommate lives here and we are close friends. There are several women that I am very close to. Next, I'm beginning to plan for the transition for when I retire. After that, there will be piano playing, maybe lessons. I've thought about learning to play the harp, organizing a book club, and some other things ....

Madeline Gee, a Woman of Stature

Standing tall, slender and with dignified and proud posture.
White hair curling close to her face
She speaks quickly, without hesitation.
One soon recognizes that this is
Madeline Gee, a woman of stature.

In her ninety and five years, there is a lot she has seen.
Large schools and small, segregated and integrated.
She talks of teaching "her children."
She taught them. She loved them.
Madeline Gee, a teacher of stature.

Her religion is her foundation.
Not only the scriptures but also its music.
She wears the cross, and knows its teachings.
She says that a chorus of her friend's prayers enable her to drive.
Madeline Gee, a parishioner of stature.

For her, life has been school and children and classrooms.
It was also community, and the arts and celebrations.
She is out and among all people, living her beliefs.
The whole community, especially its children now grown, salute
Madeline Gee, a woman of stature.

Madeline Gee

She was a teacher before and during the desegregation of schools of Williamsburg. Madeline is recognized as a devoted leader, community servant and church member as well. There are few people in Williamsburg who don't know her and she "loves them all."

Madeline Johns Gee
Born July 25, 1907

I was born into a lucky family in Portsmouth, Virginia. There were six children (three boys and three girls) in our family, and we were smart, not always honor roll people, but we weren't failures, most of us have graduated from college. My parents were our mentors — they taught us just about everything, and the neighbors kept an eye on us, too. In those days neighbors played a big part in your life; if they caught you doing something wrong, "I'll tell your parents, honey."

Because my mother died when I was nine years old, my father was the one who raised us and saw that we became good citizens. My father was a Navy man who traveled to China and other places. Here in Virginia, he was stationed at the Navy Yard in Norfolk and then had a civil service job in the area.

My father and his newspapers...! He read a lot of them and taught us to read from them; it also taught us awareness of world happenings. He did the same thing with the radio - he would say, "Listen and learn." On weekends our family drove to different places in Virginia, so that we would learn geography and become more aware of our surroundings.

I remember our dining room table where a lot went on as we sat around it; for one thing, my parents made sure we ate correctly; used the proper eating utensils; learned our manners; and did our school lessons on time. My father learned math at that table while he taught us, too. Parents, today, need to do the same thing - have fun and spend time helping your children.

When my father remarried, he brought his new wife, Annie, into our home, a new stepmother. She didn't know much about children, but she was the sweetest person! It didn't tear me to pieces because my father remarried; I often used this as an example to my students who complained about new stepmothers. I told them to give them a chance; they might find they are sweet and loving, too, like Annie.

I met my husband John in Eden (Martinsville, now), Virginia at a wedding. He was taking classes in Florida. John asked me to take him for a ride in my 1930 car (I was so proud of that car!) and he proposed to me, in that same car. He said, "You are in home-making and I am in agriculture; we'd make a good pair." We drove to my stepmother's house in Portsmouth (my father had already passed away) for permission to marry, and she told him if he treated me all right, it would be okay. (I was hiding upstairs while listening to the conversation.)

I always knew that I would be a teacher; God put me here to teach. After high school, I went to Hampton Institute (now called Hampton University) where I received a Bachelor of Science degree in Home Economics. Later, I wanted to teach science, too, so I took additional science classes at Columbia University in New York. (The College of William and Mary and other colleges in the area didn't offer the classes I needed at the time.) I taught in many public schools in the area, and I was the first African-American teacher to come to Williamsburg to integrate the school system. I'm so glad I did that because I love Williamsburg - everybody has been so good to me.

I had fun with my students, especially my eight graders! One of my students, an African-American boy, was failing his classes. But the one thing he enjoyed was playing drums - he was good, too. I encouraged him to learn everything he could about drums; this led to further learning. Eventually, he went to college, still beating his drums, and graduated with a high grade point average.

You know the proudest thing I ever did before I retired? I made sure my students improved their vocabularies. Some children were not taught definitions in classes - too many of them copied directly from the book. Well, my students used index cards and learned to use the words in a sentence; they did better on their tests.

There was a time in my life when I was shut out because of the color of my skin. In the early 40's, I wanted to be baptized as a Roman Catholic, but no one would baptize me. Finally, Father Michael, a white priest from St. Bede, said he would like to, so on a Saturday he baptized me in an all black church in Portsmouth. I just found *My Sunday Missal*, dated 1942, which Father Michael inscribed with this message: "In memory of your Baptism and First Communion," signed, "Father Michael, Christmas 1942." I truly loved that man.

Later, I moved to Williamsburg, where I started going to St. Bede's. But I missed a choir. You see, in my life your hymns were prayers. So I formed a choir of both black and white folks, and we had a good time. I was St. Bede's first organist; Father Carr and the church have been so good to me.

I want to tell young women, "Follow God's rules; respect your parents and yourself. No one will respect you if you don't care about yourself." If you are having problems, at least try to talk with them.

I've been active in many organizations in my community; I've enjoyed every one of them, and I think I helped others. But my greatest joy and accomplishment was teaching. I see my past students, occasionally, and they tell me they remember what a good teacher I was, that means a lot to me. Many of their pictures are all around my house. Not having children, these are my "children," along with my nephew Monty who is like a son to me.

A Commanding Presence, with Joyfulness. This is Judy.

Her tall, statuesque bearing is at once noted.
Beautiful white hair simply coiffed. Sensible metal rimmed glasses
Surround her bright, expressive eyes.
A commanding presence, with joyfulness. This is Judy.

Her military career as a Marine is reflected from head to toe.
Conversation about her dreams reveals a life long interest in books, reading.
Her broad, contagious smile and rich laughter shows her love of life.
A commanding presence, with joyfulness. This is Judy.

Having had the equivalent of two careers, she continues with many activities.
Serving on Boards, library committees, and leadership positions of all sorts.
But the personal caring, assisting with friends and with those less capable
illuminates yet another facet of her life. This too is Judy.

Patriotism going back to World War II is still important to her.
As is the spiritual reality of needing a relationship with a Supreme Being.
Past age 80, keeping physically fit and mentally stimulated are also priorities.
A commanding presence, with joyfulness. This is Judy.

Judy Hamblet

Achieving the highest rank for a female officer available at the time in the U.S. Marine Corps, she also became the youngest woman appointed as director of one of the U.S. Women's Military Services. After retirement she went on to the U.S. Department of Education.

Judith Hamblet

Born May 12, 1915

Born in Massachusetts and raised in New England, I found Williamsburg had much to offer retirees: Colonial Williamsburg, the College of William and Mary, a vibrant, non-industrial community and, for the most part, a gentle climate. I moved here in 1986 and for the past 17 of my 87 years, have enjoyed living at Williamsburg Landing, a continuing care retirement community. Auditing classes at William and Mary, taking courses at the Christopher Wren Association for Lifelong Learning, volunteering for 10 years at the Regional Library, and serving on the Williamsburg Landing Residents' Board and its Finance, Maintenance and Library Committees have kept me challenged and busy.

I went to Vassar, majoring in Economics. In the fall of 1937, I obtained a job at the U.S. Information Service in Washington, D.C. When World War II broke out, my two older brothers entered the military, one in the Navy and one in the Army. By 1943, I, too, decided to serve my country, and not wanting to be partial to either brother, joined the Marine Corps (which turned out to be a very fortunate decision for me).

I was the first woman Officer Candidate in the Marine Corps. Upon graduating from Officer Training School, I was commissioned a 1st Lieutenant and assigned to recruit training. By the end of the war, I was a Major and Commanding Officer of the largest Woman Marine command. My responsibilities included the "mental, moral and physical well-being" of 2,500 women on an aviation base with 20,000 men. At the time, it didn't faze me; in retrospect, it does.

When I got out of service, one of my brothers was living in London and I decided to go to the London School of Economics under the GI Bill. Shortly after arriving in London, I received a letter from the Commandant of the Marine Corps inviting me to return to active duty and head up the post-war Women's Reserve. For two years I served as Director, Marine Corps Women's Reserve.

In 1948, Congress passed the Women's Armed Services Act which made it possible for women to serve in the Regular services (not just the Reserve). I accepted a commission in the Marine Corps and, in 1953, was appointed the Director, Women Marines and promoted to colonel. For six years I served as Director, the youngest woman appointed as Director of one of the U.S. Women's service and served longer in that position than any other woman.

Following my tour as Director, I served at the NATO Southern Command Headquarters in Naples, Italy. Then to Parris Island, South Carolina where I finished my 22 year military career as Commanding Officer of the Women's Recruit Training. In 1965, when I asked a recruit why she had joined the Marine Corps, she stated, "My mother served under you and thought I should have the same experience." I knew it was time for me to retire.

My mother, for her time, was a quite modern and liberal woman and was proud of my career in the Marine Corps. I do not believe, however, that she was completely comfortable with the fact that the only Hamblet ever to make a career of the military was her daughter.

I had long been interested in education. In the fall of 1965, I joined the U.S. Office of Education and for the next seven years served in an administrative capacity in a variety of federally sponsored education programs.

I have never considered myself a feminist, though others have. I personally have not felt discriminated against, nor have I experienced any real harassment (perhaps the women in my generation took themselves a little less seriously in this regard than the women of today-or maybe I was just very lucky).

Since 9/11, many people have been living in fear. I will not. Instead, I look around me and see, feel and draw strength from the beauty of nature, art, music and literature. It's great to be an octogenarian!

Willetta, the Reverend Heising

Wearing a bright red shirt with rows of elephants, African animals.
The clerics collar rising up like the supportive stem of a flower.
A large, decorated, pewter cross resting gently between folds.
This is Willetta, the Reverend Heising.

Her soft white hair surrounds a youthful, vibrant face.
With a clear and steady gaze, she takes in every detail.
In serious discussions, intelligence and wit mix. Then a smile.
This is Willetta, the Reverend Heising.

Her story is a rich combination of scholar, mother, wife, pioneer.
Advocate for women, Hospice for the dying, racial understanding,
To know God's will, find a way to do it, until it's done.
This is Willetta, the Reverend Heising.

She was an only child, is a mother of five, a grandmother to nine.
As "the queen of the universe", she is determined, caring.
A teacher of the Bible, an activist for social justice, a seeker.
This is Willetta, the Reverend Heising.

Now at eighty, the quest continues.
Working for common ground, sometimes she uses singing.
"Why am I here?" she asked. Williamsburg, is all the better.
Because of Willetta, the Reverend Heising.

Rev. Willetta Heising

Growing up as an only child, she is mother to five and grandmother to many. Willetta also had time to become one of the first women ordained to the ministry in the Evangelical Lutheran Church.

Willetta Brand DeGood Heising

Born July 1, 1922

My mother and I spent summers with three grandparents who had a lot to do with my upbringing. I was the only granddaughter among several grandsons and was the "queen of the universe." My maternal grandfather, in particular, was a mentor to me. This grandfather was a doctor in a town in Washington state where I went with him on house calls. I remember that his presence alone made a difference to the patients he went to see. He was special because he took time with me.

Mother, who divorced a year after my birth in Estacada, Oregon and I moved to Prosser, Washington right across the river. She went to college to become a teacher and remarried when I was twelve years old. Her new husband John and I had a great deal of difficulty the first year, probably because we were so much alike. We had the same temper and he said, "My temper should not cost you what my temper cost me." I was very lucky; he became a good father to me.

Another mentor was Dr. Martin, the Political Science Department Head at the University of Washington, who encouraged me in my studies. (Before going to college in 1941 Pearl Harbor happened, so my father thought it would be good insurance for me to go to business school, which I did, for two years in case I had to start earning a living sooner than I had planned. Everything was so tenuous then.) I met my husband Ken, who was in the Navy, a year before graduating from college. We were married after I graduated in 1946 and had three girls and two boys. Watching them grow and interact with each other was exciting (remember, I was an only child). We were moving a lot, but there was a great deal of support from the Navy. (You have to have a friend.)

After Ken's Navy career, we moved to Connecticut where we were close to Yale University. (Earlier in my life I went on an ecumenical retreat where I first met a woman priest. This made a big impression on me.) In Connecticut, I began meeting with lay women "deaconesses" and went with them one day on errands. One stop was to go to the Yale Divinity School to get their grades, and I came out with an application (God was pushing!). I took the three years at Yale for my Masters of Divinity, then we moved here. I was under the supervision of the vicarage of St. Stephen's Lutheran Church to complete the requirements for ordination. I did a clinical pastoral internship at Eastern State Hospital in Williamsburg (400 plus hours). It was wonderful. What moved me the most was the kindness of the staff there. Most of them viewed their work as a "calling."

In order to be ordained you must have a church. However, being a woman and wanting to become ordained was an obstacle. The Missouri Synod Lutheran Church wouldn't ordain a woman and still doesn't. The Association of Evangelical Lutheran Churches, of which I am a member, split off from the Missouri Synod. I was appointed to a parish in Franklin, Virginia where I was ordained on my 59th birthday, the first woman whom my bishop had ever ordained. (Now the three large Lutheran churches have merged and it is different.) Later I went to Union Seminary in Richmond for a year's program in religion.

When we moved to Williamsburg, I wondered what was in mind for me. There was no hospice program, nothing for domestic violence and the racial situation was difficult. I had a hand in starting both Hospice and Avalon (a shelter for battered women and their children). I've had a Bible study class for years, first in St. Stephens and then in our home where I continue to teach.

I would tell young women that they must be careful in life. When I was growing up, I was never concerned for my safety. I was secure within the circle of family and community. I am fearful for my grandchildren who do not have this safety and security. Why do we need a shelter for battered women in every community? Young women need to take care of themselves. If they don't have family, then create one. Form a network for personal safety and support.

Now that I'm eighty, I've been reading about one of the things one must do turning eighty years old. One must figure out what the next period of life is going to be. I'm working on that right now. I'd like to add that, besides God's help, I've had Ken's support and love, my husband of 56 years.

Loving, Lovely ... Lois

Clothes of purple, lavender, smooth silk, coarsely woven tweed, blue denim.
She is tall with a statuesque carriage learned years ago for modeling clothes.
Her voice has the quality of someone who sings.
Measured and firm but with a bit of twinkle when appropriate.
Graceful and composed, she is connected in mind, body and spirit.

Some thoughts were spontaneous, but there were also jottings she read having
Pondered carefully the questions we asked.
Smiling, a light seems to glimmer from within.
There is no hesitation or doubt in her words.
Perhaps because they come either from experience, or directly from her soul.
Beauty and compassion, travel and family, each corner and wall is filled with
Personal mementos and lively memorabilia. The surroundings are like a set upon
Which their family lives are played out. Decorations such as elegant top hats and
Derbies used to greet arriving family at the airport add whimsy, fun.

Involvement in and activities in the community are too numerous to be listed
And her life's work. Knowing, serving the spirit of God is her foundation.

Lois, lovely and loving.

Lois Hornsby

Music, love of family and service to God were a part of her early life. In a myriad of civic organizations, large and small; Lois continues to be a "backbone" to her familiy and to the Williamsburg community.

Lois Saunier Hornsby

I was born a Depression baby, but my parents knew they had a special charge, so they imparted a good sense of New England thrift and common sense to me. In doing that, they gave me a special gift. It helped so much with my attitude about life and people. They came to Virginia during World War I. My father's assignment was as an entertainer; he was a fine musician. His mother was a concert pianist who fell in love with a Baptist minister, so she left the concert stage and went into church music. She helped my father learn as he worked his way through Brown University as the organist and choir director at a big Baptist church in Providence, Rhode Island. That's where he met my mother.

My mother was one in a large family who were a great group. We'd go back and visit in the summer. They imparted just a wonderful sense of community to me, and a sense of finding a reason for being, for taking up space here and what you can bring to the community. My mother was always active in the Parent Teacher Association (PTA), the League of Women Voters, the church, etc. All of these made so much sense to me, and I could see the results and the differences it made. That's how I came to enjoy helping people. My mother became a Christian Scientist because her best friend's mother was a Christian Science Practitioner whose spirituality and beliefs were discussed at length with her. My father was supportive of her belief in Christian Science. When my parents moved south, my mother was told she would be an invalid for the rest of her life but, through prayer and her beliefs, she became one of the healthiest, strongest persons I had ever known. Furthermore, she was told she would never have any children and there, again, I came on the scene.

My dad was born in Nyack, New York but served in Petersburg, Virginia in WWI. He was wooed to Richmond by an offer from St. James Episcopal Church, next door to a synagogue, so he was organist at both of those places. Then he was music minister at Second Baptist Church for 40 plus years with an interim at Monument Methodist near Lee Circle on Monument Avenue. I became so appreciative of all worship places, and how most had the same basis of the Golden Rule, which is certainly what makes life work.

I have one brother, my only sibling, who is eight years older than I. He helped a lot of my thinking, too. He subscribed early on to the *New Yorker* for me and was active in politics and desegregation.

I was never as aware of segregation (the whole concept was just surprising to me) as when I was a young married woman. We had two fine black housekeepers to help take care of the children. I could never understand why they wouldn't really look at me. I came to understand they felt they weren't supposed to look someone in the eye, for that would be considered presumptuous.

I learned so much from the people who worked for us, and I got to know them as people. I advise parents to get to know their kids. They need to learn what their children are learning and to become involved in their activities. The PTA is one of the many parental activities they can take part in.

I so treasure my parents. It is true that the daughter is greatly influenced by her mother. However, when I hear about child abuse, I'm so grateful and have so much more respect for my father ... I realize how blessed I was to have a father who really protected me, and I just had such a nice relationship with him.

I really think the Sermon on the Mount, the life and words and works of Jesus, are my basis for action 'cause I think I've learned really not to rely on the advice of people, except for my family, for people come and go and they can disappoint you at times. But the Almighty Creator of all never disappoints for guidance.

The biggest influence, outside of my birth family, was my husband who was so unselfish and supportive. He would encourage me in all the things I was involved in. I was a fashion model in Richmond before and after we were married and I helped Casey's Department Store for many years with fashion coordination. I had thought I would go into the merchandising business, but I decided to get married instead. In those days married women who didn't have to work, didn't. However, for five years I was a hostess for Colonial Williamsburg at the Governor's Palace. Then the babies, Robert, Bruce and Jonathan, came and home was the center.

I believe in exposing young people to Shakespeare's language and all the wonderful learning that comes with it. It was thought that a bridge could be built between the Shakespearean Festival of the college and the community. The actress Helen Hayes was our first honorary chair for the Festival. I hope the Williamsburg story reflects what I've tried to be, really what we all should try to be. It was one of respect for the individual and cooperation. I think that the Williamsburg story is what I have believed in as part of America, a land where there is freedom, self-reliance, and mutual respect. (Unfortunately, freedom was not extended to many of the African-Americans in the beginning.)

I advise young women to cherish their future and not just live for today. You want to be proud that you respected your body and yourself. Also, to give to your community. There's so much you can do, even if it's just one thing, you'll feel good about it.

Now I continue to work for the community: public education; All Together (the understanding of all races); the Clergy Fellowship; the Shakespeare Festival, the College of William and Mary; and my relatives. Hopefully a Williamsburg Botanical Garden is in the future, with the Nature Conservatory.

Small by nature, but what a voice!

Seated comfortably in a studio with a grand piano surrounded by
Book and record shelves on all three walls, she deftly leads the conversation.
Her dark, expressive eyes are framed with clearly arched eyebrows.
Dark hair ("my own, you know") cropped at ear length swings easily.
Small by nature, but what a voice!

As Genevieve tells her story, her hands add emphasis to ideas, thoughts of all kinds.
It is not difficult to visualize those strong movements leading a chorus.
The strength, tone and ability to project her voice is evident even in this room;
The sound in an auditorium or concert hall is easy to imagine.

She takes her listener through the travels of theatres, universities, opera
Companies, choruses of many different kinds.
It is a journey sometimes down the back roads and at other times on the main
Highways of American music. Almost always spiced with the classics.

Travels to many continents and countries are reflected in wall pieces.
Simple quilting from a rural crafter, a finished piece by an artist sculpted in stone,
Woven masks from tribal teachers.
Hers is a lifetime of sharing her gifts, teaching and cultivating other's talents.
The parents who were her teachers taught her well.
Small by nature, but what a voice!

Genevieve McGiffert

Daughter of two teachers, it was no surprise that Genevieve also became a part of the education system. Her special niche was music of all kinds and she performed, taught, directed and created a variety of programs for whatever community in which she lived.

Genevieve White McGiffert
Born September 4, 1926

I grew up in West Virginia, about 25 miles north of Charleston. There were few "extras" in my life, but I was tremendously lucky because both my parents were teachers; my father became a superintendent of schools. My parents were highly respected in West Virginia and loved by their students. We had little money, but during my childhood, the period of the Great Depression, few people did. Both my parents were poor as young people, but they completed their college degrees after I was born. Not many people in that area of West Virginia had degrees.

My mother went back to teaching when I was one month old. She would come home from school to breast feed me. She was more of a teacher to me than a mother. When I grew older, she advised me not to marry right away but to get more education. My father's philosophy of education was, "Teach them to read, then they read to learn." Most important about teaching, I can hear him say, "Set'em on fire and then get out of the way!" My parents were a major influence on me. They loved to teach and were extremely interested in how well their students learned. This had a lasting effect on my own interest in teaching and in helping other people realize their potential. They were my role models.

Mostly relatives were my caregivers when my mother returned to teaching. At age three, I had a severe case of whooping cough and, when recovering, I was asked what I would like - a doll, a book? I asked to go to school. So at age four, I was permitted to go to school with my mother who was teaching in a small one-room school. One or the other of my parents was my teacher through the seventh grade. Making high grades was very important so I stayed pretty focused on learning. That's how I graduated from high school at age 15 as valedictorian in a class of 100. I went to the Cincinnati Conservatory of Music at the age of 16, and at 19 I graduated with Bachelor of Music degrees in piano and voice. A couple of years later, I finished my Master of Music degree in voice.

Cincinnati was a very musical city. Because the city had a strong German concentration, famous lieder artists, such as the great Lotte Lehmann, came frequently to perform. The Cincinnati Symphony was world famous. In the summer there was an opera festival using Metropolitan Opera conductors, singers and chorus. I not only was the beneficiary of these superb musical events, but I got to perform in small parts a couple of times at the opera festival called the "Zoo Opera," because the performances were mounted on an outdoor stage at the Cincinnati Zoo.

Lucy Jackson, my private voice teacher, was my mentor when I was young. I started studying with her when I was nine years old. She was a graduate of Juilliard and set high standards. She took me to concerts of great artists on the Community Concert

Series in Charleston. She guided my training for the Conservatory, which led me into singing, piano, opera and, eventually, acting and directing.

It's difficult to answer what my biggest accomplishment is, because whatever I'm doing at the time is my favorite. I love accompanying and coaching singers, conducting operas and musicals, and acting. My fondness for performance began early in my life when my first "acting" was reciting "The Bear Story" by James Whitcomb Riley. There were frequent performances as an actress, singer and pianist in high school and college.

At the end of World War II, the Conservatory needed teachers because there was a great influx of students on the GI Bill of Rights. I taught while finishing my Master's in voice. Then my teachers moved to New York City, and I went with them as their studio coach/accompanist and to study further. I was determined to enter the opera world, but so soon after the war there was very little opportunity. Thriving regional opera developed much later. So, in 1952, after studying in New York City for three years, I married a philosophy professor at Colgate University.

At that time, Colgate was a men's school and all the faculty positions were filled by men. But they needed women as actresses, so I acted in many roles in their theatre productions of Shakespeare, Shaw, Maugham and Christopher Fry, among others. Another enterprising woman conductor began a Gilbert and Sullivan Society and I sang the leading soprano roles. In addition, I went to Syracuse University for a Master's in Education, taught in public schools and directed plays of Wilder and Anouilh, as well as operettas. In 1960, after a divorce and remarriage, my new husband, Dr. Michael McGiffert, a history professor, was hired by the University of Denver. Though there was no immediate position for me, by the second year I was hired on the voice and opera faculty. In all cases I adapted and found interesting opportunities to use my training and experience.

I've been married twice; no children. My first husband, Dr. Theodore Mischel, was a Jewish refugee from the Anschluss in Austria. I enjoyed the experience of participating in Jewish family life. My mother-in-law complimented me by calling me a "Mench" (in Yiddish usage, a sympathetic and humane person). My husband's intellectual and social contacts were challenging and stimulating. Unfortunately, this marriage mostly centered around his interests, not mine. We divorced in the late 50's and settled matters amicably. My second marriage has lasted 43 years. I am lucky because many people I know with successful careers have not been able to sustain marriages. One reason is that professional singers and conductors must travel constantly in order to advance their careers. Though my present husband, a Colonial American historian and the retired editor of *The William and Mary Quarterly*, and I lead separate professional lives, we try to be together as much as we can; for example, have all our meals together daily. We have traveled all over the world.

There have been many turning points. As a person with a career, my life has always changed when I changed geographic locations, and I've had to adjust to pursuing the jobs available to me. For example, when my second husband was appointed to the faculty of the University of Denver and there was no position for me, I made myself useful as a private vocal coach in art song and actress in plays of Schiller, Macleish, Arthur Miller and others, and by the second year a position opened up.

Normand Lockwood became the composer-in-residence in 1960 also. He composed three new operas in the next five years. I sang the soprano-leading role in one and conducted the premieres of the other two. It was a fascinating experience to work on untried compositions with a distinguished composer. Within a couple of years I became head of the voice faculty and head of the opera department. During the following 10 years, I conducted and staged many full opera productions and opera workshop concerts. The major productions we presented were by composers Mozart, Puccini, Rossini, Britten, Offenbach, Floyd, Menotti and others.

Denver University (D.U.) had a historic connection to the Central City Opera Festival, and I became director of the Central City Opera Workshop for apprentices. An assistant conductor, one of the leading singers, and I directed the young apprentices, many of whom are successful professional singers today, in opera scenes. As time went on, I got my Ph.D. in theatre from D.U., combining music and theatre in my dissertation on the musico-dramatic techniques of Benjamin Britten's great opera Peter Grimes.

The 1960's was the initial period of development for Young Audiences programs, where professional singers and instrumentalists, supported by the National Endowment for the Arts, were sent into the public schools. I was a participant in Young Audiences in Colorado and continued this kind of program under the aegis of the Virginia Opera later.

Perhaps the biggest challenge occurred thirty years ago when my husband was hired as editor of The William and Mary Quarterly and we moved to Williamsburg. The College of William & Mary was not a place for professional singers to be trained, as we had at the University of Denver. When I explored different musical opportunities, the Virginia Opera was just beginning and I worked with them as their chorus master for the next three years. During the last year I lectured around the state about the U. S. premiere of Mary, Queen of Scots by Thea Musgrave. One of my functions was again to participate in Young Audiences. Soon, owing to my visibility at the Virginia Opera, I had established a professional identity of sorts. We invested in property in Virginia Beach so I would have a studio for singers from Tidewater cities, and within a couple of years I was able to maintain a full schedule of private teaching. I was privileged to work with many promising talents, some of whom won major recognition and prizes; many others continue to be regional soloists; and some are successful teachers. Eventually traveling back and forth to Norfolk became a problem, so I focused my work in Williamsburg. I have always had to adjust to different situations and to new people. It was a challenge and I did my best to meet it.

In 1989 a group of Unitarian Universalists (U.U.) were reorganizing to focus on liberal religious values in the city of Williamsburg. I became a charter member and devoted much attention and time to those early efforts as a member of the board of directors in planning and advising on the construction of a new church, and in building a choir. The choir became an important part of the U.U. service, and I remained as its director until 1995, when I resigned because of other responsibilities.

From 1993 through 1999, I served as the Artistic Director/Conductor of the Williamsburg Choral Guild until the end of 1999. We preformed some of the great oratorio repertoire, and the last year involved me in the celebration of the Tricentennial of the town of Williamsburg when the Guild presented three major historical concerts. Even though I retired from the Guild at the end of the Tricentennial, Guild members and the organization are still dear to my heart. The following year I established a non-profit arts organization, "Art Song of Williamsburg," whose mission is "to further the art of solo song by presenting great vocal literature of the Western world to Williamsburg area audiences." I could have started "Art Song" fifteen years ago, but there is now a growing core of culturally sophisticated people who are fertile ground for a person like me to introduce what I love doing.

As a professional musician, being a woman has been only a minor obstacle. Frankly, I think it is wonderful to be a woman! An example of difficulty for a short while occurred at the University of Denver. In the 1960's, colleges and universities did not like to hire and promote two members of the same family. But after a few years as an instructor, I was eventually promoted and when I left the university I was an associate professor. Women's issues, like that one, were much more restrictive forty years ago.

As a female conductor, I had no problems, but that was probably because I was in academia. I was not competing with men for a professional position. There were no women orchestral or opera conductors at the helm of major professional organizations in those days. Also, I am of Anglo-Saxon stock and am white, so I had none of the handicaps so many people have had. My mother was what you might call today an early feminist. She started teaching school at 18 and took off only one year for a second pregnancy. From the beginning of my childhood, my parents urged education, not immediate marriage and a family. "Anyone can do that," my mother said.

As far as advice to the next generation is concerned, I would say, "Inspire by precept and example; that is a lot better than giving advice. I have had students who were gifted and could have had brilliant careers, but they didn't make the choice to stay with it long enough. It is really difficult to become a professional singer - it takes time, commitment, extensive learning, discipline, and good health. For example, there was one young woman who came to me for voice lessons. She had a truly remarkable talent but didn't follow through with her career. Another young woman, who was her competitor early on but was not as advanced at the time, has persevered and is now singing at the New York City Opera and the Metropolitan Opera. If you plan on a musical career, early marriage may not be in the picture. There are a lot of moves and changes." Most of all, I would advise everyone to stay healthy. The older you get, the more important it becomes.

I'd like to continue what I'm doing and that includes more traveling abroad. My husband and I have traveled extensively in Europe, and visited China (2000) and India (2001). I would deteriorate quickly if I didn't have a challenging opportunity. I'm just not a tea drinker or a shopper. Right now, I have to deal with high blood pressure, so I have to work on staying healthy.

Barbara of Sussex House, Richmond Road

The rectangular brick house usually has an open front door.
The large dining room has held many guests at its long table.
Political notables being entertained.
City officials, business associates and family, friends, strangers.
Hostess, Barbara, orchestrates it all.

Her dark eyes move almost as quickly as she talks.
Thoughts and ideas are expressed in staccato fashion
As if to pause, she might lose the beat.
Willing to take a risk, she was often the "first" woman,
Businesswoman, Barbara, speaks with assurance.

All the achievements, awards and accolades, the list is long.
Being mother of three children, she describes with the most pride.
Always busy and active, they were what fueled the action.
A softness creeps into her authoritative voice.
Daughter and mother, Barbara, is grounded by relationships.
Barbara of Sussex House, Richmond Road

Barbara Collins Baganakis

Out of need to support her family, she entered the real estate world (which was mostly male) with energy and the ability to compete successfully. Barbara was a business woman, political activist and the first woman leader of the Williamsburg Chamber of Commerce.

Barbara Collins Baganakis

Born January 12, 1935

My family, according to my husband Johnny, was the most stable family he had ever heard about in his entire life. I grew up in one house with parents who stayed married to each other, had a brother and sister, attended one school system, knew all four grandparents and lived so close to one set that I visited them daily and the other set on Sundays. This was in southwestern Virginia where I grew up in the Appalachian Mountain area. Really, I'm a "hick." But we were not totally backwoods people. We were poor but we didn't know it. There were many generations of my family in this locale and my interest and work in genealogy has brought a whole lot of information about our family going back many generations. I was influenced by my whole family. We are strong people, for we were close to one another and strong individually.

I was married three times. In my first marriage, I lived all over West Virginia for my husband installed for the telephone company. We divorced and by that time I had two children, one was just two and a half months old when we separated. I went back to Virginia Tech, and my maternal grandmother took care of the children while I went to school. I remarried (by the way, I am on good terms with both my former husbands), had a daughter, and moved to Richmond. In 1964, the family moved to Williamsburg where my husband worked for WBCl, the local radio station. I went into real estate before they had schools so I prepared for the exam on my own. Soon Larry McCardle, a Williamsburg realtor, wanted me to open an agency with him. I went to Marshall Wythe Law School at William and Mary and took all the courses I could dealing with real estate. I took courses in contract law, things like that, so I have about one year's worth of law school. Knowing lots of people helped, and the school wasn't as stringent then about who was taking courses.

Even though I had three children, I wanted a career of my own. There definitely was a financial desire. I wanted to have enough money to educate the children and have a nice life style. However, this meant that I missed some of the important things of their young lives. My son was a terrific athlete, and I remember his asking me one time what was for dinner. I told him that I wasn't quite sure what the Motor House Restaurant was serving that night, but I assured him that it would be good. We ate out a lot because I was working all the time. Real estate business is very demanding of your time, weekends included. Also, it taught my son to be independent. Nothing wrong with that because it made him a better husband for his wife.

My greatest accomplishment was raising three great kids. They all turned out well and that's an accomplishment! Also, marrying my third husband Johnny Baganakis was one of the best things I ever did.

I haven't looked at anything as an obstacle. It is more an "opportunity." Being a female has had its problems, especially in business. It is still a problem in this country to this day. When we had the agency, I would answer the phone and callers would want to talk with Mr. Murphy. When they found out there was no Mr. Murphy, they asked to speak with Mr. McCardle.

My activity in politics began with my becoming a raving Republican after being raised a Democrat. The Republican Committee convinced me to oppose State Representative George Grayson in an election. I decided to run for the House of Delegates in 1979 and put everything on hold for six months. I did nothing but campaign; unfortunately, I lost but the man was undefeated. Also, I became a good friend of John Warner during the days when he was married to Elizabeth Taylor, and Johnny and I entertained them here at some big parties.

I've had some firsts in my life; for example, owning a portion of a real estate company. There were few women in the field at that time, but I never let this stand in my way. I've always felt this: men put their pants on the same way that I do. That's a fact. Also, locally, I was the first woman president of the Williamsburg Chamber of Commerce (1983), and I have been active in the Soroptomist Club, a member of the Virginia Citizen Planning Association, appointed to the Planning Commission for the City of Williamsburg, active on the Wetlands Board, campaigned for several governors, etc.

Every morning I face each day by "putting on my boots" for whatever I have to do, whether it's to walk, run or meet a business appointment. You do it whether you feel like it or not. That's where I get my strength.

I am sad because I've lost my husband. He was sick for a long time. Maybe I can do some things that I didn't have an opportunity to do before, like taking care of myself physically. As I grieve, I write family stories to keep myself sane and to keep on going. I have also done a lot of genealogy, which I have so much fun with.

I would say to young women: "Don't let anything stand in your way of doing what you really want to do. At the same time, try not to miss too much of your children's lives. It goes so fast. If you make a mistake in marriage, a job, or are doing anything wrong, get out of it, change it, do something about it."

Mildred, Sweet Mildred

You have much to tell us. There is so much for us to learn.
From your walks to school, oh such long walks as the bus carrying white
Children passed you by
To the school where you taught and the heat was by wood stove.
The boys cut the wood and the girls cooked the peas.
You have much to tell us. There is so much for us to learn.

Your Daddy made sure you all went down the dirt road to the Church.
Years later, at his own time, he joined you.
Those walks down that road were free and happy on the way
But later on, when the sun was going down, the "hangin' tree" stood out
Stark against the setting sun. A scary place it was.
You have much to tell us. There is so much for us to learn.

You had to leave home to enter Denbigh High School. It was country then.
You graduated, then went on to Hampton Institute to become a teacher.
To help other people, to be of service. You knew what you wanted to be.
To work with your sister, to be nourished, to learn and to be yourself.
You found a mansion and a family to serve. It was also a place of love.
You have much to tell us. There is so much for us to learn.

Eight decades and more, you have served your God.
Small in frame, light of weight, but solid and strong.
Twinkling and bright, intelligent and firmly planted.
Your brown face crinkles with pleasure and delight
At the questions, the stories you tell.
You have much to tell us. There is so much for us to learn.

Mildred, Sweet Mildred.

Mildred Redcross

It was the early days of segregated schools when she had to move in with relatives in order to attend high school. Decades of teaching and taking care of children makes Mildred known and loved by many in our community today.

Mildred Jarvis Redcross
November 22, 1912 - June 24, 2003

I had two brothers and a sister. My mother was daddy's second wife. Daddy made sure that we went to Sunday School and church, but he himself didn't start going to church until he was in his 50's - it just wasn't his time. On Sunday, all of us children dressed in our best clothes, walked the one-mile dirt road to church, stayed there all morning, and walked back home for lunch. We'd put on playclothes and then walk back again, but this would be later in the afternoon when the sun was going down. It was scary to walk past the "hangin' tree" where Negroes were once hanged. You see, one night we saw someone hanging there - oh, yes, we did in our imaginations! I remember how scared we were.

My parents wanted us to get an education, but the money was scarce. My cousin Amanda, who owned two convalescent homes in Newport News, took me into her home. I lived there from my high school days through my graduation in 1947 from Hampton Institute (Hampton University, now) with a Masters Degree in Elementary Education. Amanda raised and supported me, financially and emotionally. Without her, I never would have had such an opportunity. She was my mentor!

While living with my cousin, I worked at a mansion with my sister who learned to be a nurse by taking correspondence courses. We worked everyday after school and in the summers. This huge house was in Yorktown, you know, the one right across from the statue. We were in charge of setting the table, caring for the linens and doing other tasks. We did everything because there was always something going on at that house.

When I started teaching, my favorite school was Frederick Douglass Elementary (Griffin Yates, now). There was good interaction among the principal, staff and children. The Parent Teacher Association was active; I could visit problem children in their homes, something I often did. Now you wouldn't be able to do that. I retired from Waller Mill Elementary in 1977 after 39 years of teaching.

I took my only child, Ann, on those parent visits. We'd drive down some bumpy backroads and often got lost. We'd call my husband Raymond who would come and rescue us on his 1941 motorcycle (smile), or give us phone directions on how to get back home.

Ann said to tell you how my ex-pupils say I helped them THINK and that has helped them get to where they are today (many have done well).

Over the years Raymond, Ann and I traveled extensively — we went to Europe in 1973 and traveled throughout the United States. We felt it was important to educate Ann in different cultures. There were times we would travel in the deep South and Ann, just a child, wouldn't understand why we would not be allowed to stay in many motels in the city. We had to drive late into the night, sometimes, and we were tired.

I would tell young people to believe in God, like the morning star. Set your standards above everything else. Everybody has a little spark within that wants to come out.

Public schools need to put God back into schools and leave the guns out. When I was in school, we used to say the Pledge of Allegiance and have a prayer every morning. It was optional. When guns started coming into schools, God went out of them.

Colette Ringgold

She sits straight and tall. Dignified. Competent.
Her lovely white hair neat in a French braid, held by a pink ribbon.
Skin as soft as an infants and eyes that twinkle with delight.
Her accent is lightly flavored with French but easily understood.
She is a woman with wisdom to share.

Growing up in a multicultural home, she learned the ways of others.
She also learned other languages spoken by relatives and friends.
Her father was in academics, Colette followed in his footsteps.
She spent a lifetime teaching languages both in France and in the US.
She is a woman with wisdom to share.

She sees her greatest accomplishment as the mothering of two sons.
Her students see her as an extraordinary teacher.
The Society of the Blind sees her as an accomplished author.
Her friends see her as a woman of great courage, wit and stamina.
She is a woman with wisdom to share.

A stranger might see her as just a very attractive elderly woman
Friends of all ages and stages tell of her openness, inclusiveness, bright spirit.
Her smile brightens as she shares something new she's learned.
She lowers her head humbly when complimented, but shows appreciation.
She is ninety and nine years of age. A woman with wisdom to share.

Colette Ringgold

Born and raised in France, she came to the United States by herself as a young adult to teach French. She was on the faculty at the College of William and Mary, raised two sons, wrote a book and continued helping people learn languages, until her death in March 2003.

Colette Pernot Ringgold
June 21, 1903 - March 9, 2003

My mother was staunch Dutch and my father was traditional French. I had two sisters, both younger, and we grew up speaking Dutch for playing and French for academics. My sisters and I, pretending we were in a secret society, liked to speak Dutch so the French kids would hear us. Summers were spent in Holland where we visited five uncles and eleven cousins in different cities. Growing up, I remember "special cakes" and tea in the afternoon on the terrace...listening to my British teacher, who taught me English by reading children's stories... bugles signaling German bombers' approach...going to the basement.

My youngest sister Helène (nicknamed Lénio) was very active in a unit of the French Resistance during the war. She ultimately was deported by the Gestapo and starved and worked to death in Ravensbrück Concentration Camp. The second sister, Annie, lived in Paris with her large family until her death in 2002. Even up to the last year when we spoke on the telephone we spoke Dutch to each other.

My parents were liberal but also very strict. I felt loved but was expected to behave. We were raised Protestant in a Roman Catholic country which meant that we were a minority. We lived in a suburb of Paris and took the train each Sunday to the French Protestant Church for Sunday school and church. And I was one of two Protestants in the public school from ages 6-16. This didn't matter to me because I grew up with different cultures and languages. I have remained a member of the French Protestant Church in Washington, where I found many like-minded people early on in my American experience.

My parents always had foreign students visiting in our home. My father was a professor of Modern Greek at the Sorbonne where he created the Institute of Phonetics. We often had foreign students at our dinner table, so there was a lot of cultural mixture. My mother was remarkable, because like my father, she could always find room for "one more" and was interested in everyone. My parents were my mentors! I thoroughly loved and respected my father. I had the occasion to accompany him on many of his study trips to Greece, Romania and other "exotic" locations.

My mother-in-law was supportive and wonderful to me, too. During World War II when my husband was an army colonel, I spent a great deal of time visiting with his mother, along with my older son. She was the wife of a very strict and fervent Baptist minister. My mother-in-law was rigid in her religion, but she loved me and I loved her. There were times I didn't have news about my husband, and she would comfort me.

The turning points in my life were coming to the United States by myself, after I passed my baccalaureate exam in 1921, to teach French in Middlebury, Vermont (summers of 1932-42), then Wellesley College in Massachusetts (1934-1942), then here, the College of William and Mary. Those were big accomplishments for me. I came here by myself in my late 20's. I was scared but my curiosity helped me. I met my husband at Middlebury College. He was a teacher at the New York Military Academy (prep school) and took courses from me at Middlebury during the summer sessions. We had students come and go in our home, just like my parents, I continued the practice extensively after he passed away in 1988. I've always enjoyed keeping contact with foreign students or students who were serious in their studies.

I had no obstacles in my way. I'm blind from macular degeneration, but I didn't let that stop me. I have always enjoyed being helpful to others, so I followed a constructive suggestion and I dictated a book on this disease, *Out of the Corner of My Eye*. It was published by the National Association for the Blind, and is in its second or third printing. They also decided to publish it as a talking book, which is appropriate because it is directed at the visually impaired. Being blind helped me to assert myself. Before, I was shy and wouldn't always ask things. Now I do. I have found that people are very receptive to me when they realize that I have visual and hearing deficiencies, and my interaction with people has changed for the positive.

My major accomplishment was having two boys who turned out to be such fine adults. My husband of 44 years died...ah, I was head over heels in love with my husband and he was an excellent father. (She pursed her lips and blew a kiss in the air with her fingers circled to demonstrate "perfect" when she talked about her husband.) I know I could be with the boys and my wonderful daughters-in-law, but I have friends in Williamsburg and at the Landing where I live. One son, a retired Deputy Assistant Director of the FBI lives in Switzerland, and my other son, a career National Park Ranger and now the Superintendent of the Redwood National Park, in California. A grandson and a granddaughter volunteered for the Peace Corps.

I speak French with Elizabeth (Melton), a close American friend who lives here in Williamsburg. (Elizabeth met Colette through a professor who was helping her [Elizabeth] with her French. At the time, Colette was in her late 80's, and she volunteered to also help her speak French without "glitches" Elizabeth meets with her twice a week, once at the Landing and every Friday at a local restaurant where a group enjoys good food and converses in French. Elizabeth also states that Colette is a wealth of knowledge and feeling with a fine mind, not judgmental but very open-minded.) The French group has been a very positive force in my life. I enjoy interacting with them almost weekly.

The advice I give to young people is that they should be open-minded and learn other languages. When I was six, I knew two and was learning a third, English. America is new at the job of learning different languages. Everybody is short- sighted when they are out of this country. I decided to make my sons bilingual, and succeeded in that by never ever speaking English with them. I even gave them French lessons every morning before they went off to school. Knowing language helps you know people. And I've observed young women here. They're more aggressive than traditional European ones who ask their mothers first. I think, sometimes, American women should ask their mothers first (smile).

I'm never bored. I made truffles at Christmas. When I was a child, Christmas was religious; we didn't celebrate St. Nicholas. I love to read, listen to tapes and eat nutritious food. I often have afternoon tea with a friend. My sons are planning my 100th birthday party, and all my family will be here with my friends. I can't wait!

————————————

Colette died on March 9, 2003 at Woodhaven Hall, Williamsburg Landing. Her sons, Alan and Andrew, reviewed her conversation with us and made a few additions. They also added the following comments making her story more complete.

The original experiences she had in the United States were truly unique for her time. Young women didn't pack up and go to the United States the way she did. For a "shy" person it was quite an effort and an accomplishment. She often talked about the rough crossings on the ships.

Our mother went through several years as a caregiver to her husband when he was subjected to Alzheimer's disease. This was during the period when she had just lost her sight and was increasingly unable to hear. It was a very dramatic period in her life.

From her clear view the people who feel she helped them were truly helping her. She enjoyed the interaction and being able to lend assistance, but she also benefited from their assistance at the same time.

Through the "French Group" our mother met some people who were very important to her; sustaining her, entertaining her, and giving her strength when she needed it.

Barbara

Diminutive, graceful in movement, thoughtful in speech,
Barbara curled easily into the couch's softness...her foot reached out and stretched.

She located "Shachti", lowered her head and her voice to be fully present to
Her beloved pet. The cat looked up and then slowly stretched.

On the bookcase are three dramatic photos in black and white of her daughters,
Also psychologists. They have stretched out on their own.

The room is filled with paintings and sculptures and books which are like
Beautiful certificates of travel, a life fully lived, stretching east and west.

She speaks carefully, with quiet reflection but not hesitation and always, the
Thoughts developing, coming into focus, stretching farther out.

Strong, yet gentle. Positive, yet inquisitive. Searching, yet centered.
Open, yet filled. Energetic, yet calm. Stretching...always stretching.

Barbara

Barbara Rockwell

It is likely that a beloved aunt influenced her to become a therapist. Years later, after raising three girls, Barbara graduated from divinity school and is currently studying shamanism, while planning to write her second book.

Barbara Nelson Rockwell
Born December 9, 1920

There is a strain of creativity as well as melancholia genetically in our family. Life in our family was not happy. My brother, just younger than me, took care of me and I of him. Whether my mother started drinking when I was a child or later isn't clear. My father was very much in love with her, though he did try to protect me from hurtful remarks and neglect. Once my father remarked to me that the "first child is always the most special," a remark cherished for the rest of my life. There was no physical abuse, but words can hurt, and my mother was a wizard with words. In my mother's defense, she too had been a neglected child and was incapable of giving a little girl protection, which she herself had lacked.

However, my extended family living close compensated for my mother's neglect. My aunt became my role model. Not only was she a psychologist, and a world famous one, she spent a lot of time playing with me and my brothers and cousins. She often had us over for playing games. Actually my aunt was doing research, but we thought of the play as games. I loved school. My teachers gave me encouragement and school was fun and a retreat.

A therapist helped me see that my mother was jealous of me. Not surprisingly I became a psychologist, so I could help other women who were in pain. I married my first husband when we were at the University of Wyoming in Laramie, my birthplace, and he went off to war for three years overseas. When he returned we had three wonderful daughters, but divorced after 34 years of marriage, though we're still friends and talk often about our daughters. After my third child, I got my Ph.D. from George Washington University and interned at Bethesda Naval Hospital. For 20 years I had a private practice in Washington D.C. plus working at American University and the District Mental Health Clinic. Later I moved to Gloucester, Virginia where I commuted back and forth between Gloucester and D.C. finally moving my practice to Williamsburg, Virginia.

During my practice, at the time of Martin Luther King, I was fortunate to work with a group of black children in D.C. They were angry, these kids, and I tried "download" some of that anger and listen to them. In 1973 I became involved with Esalen, California, a humanistic movement and started my own program called "Arica," based upon spirituality and new psychological and experimental techniques. Two professors from John Hopkins were on our Board. I was involved with interesting and exciting people. We had well known leaders of workshops like Abraham Maslow, Fritz Perls, and Alan Watts.

When I was 70 years old, I took time from my practice to go to the Virginia Theological Seminary in Alexandria, Virginia where I received my Masters of Theological Studies. I didn't have doubts about going at this age - I wanted to do it and I did. I wanted to learn more about the Christian church. I thought as long as God put me here I might become a priest, but the committee recommended that I not seek ordination. I was angry yet had a feeling of freedom at the same time. I had already studied Hinduism with Swami Chinmayananda, and later Buddhism. I continued to search.

Meeting Swami Chinmayananda, a Hindu Master, was a real turning point in my life. My daughter had studied with him in India and it was clear the first time I saw him that he could read my mind. If I thought of a question he answered it before I could voice it. The experience was so powerful that I went to my daughter in tears. "What happened?" I asked. "Swamiji told you everything you knew and everything you didn't know," she answered.

I recommend to women they never give up searching and learning, asking, "How can we possibly change the world unless we change ourselves?" I'm still learning. I've been married twice since my first divorce. One marriage was very short and a mistake. When I married John, my present husband, I was in seminary and I remember the day he drove to Alexandria to propose, ring in hand. People love John. He has taught me about being loved and loving.

Recently, I wrote a fictional biography about my great-grandmother called *Sara's Gold.* I feel very close to her, and presently I'm thinking of another book, title yet undecided. The pioneer family I came from still directs my life. Life has had its share of excitement, success, sadness and searching.

Peg Keeps Doing the Jobs that Need to be Done.

Petite, but not fragile, she sits in a room filled with family pieces of
Distinctive boxes, handmade furniture, New England antiques.
The walls are filled with arranged pieces. Each with a story,
Reflecting some of the jobs that needed to be done.
Her light coloring blends into the bright openness.

The large, airy kitchen is where hundreds of jars of jam
Carefully labeled are prepared for the church store.
Earlier, it was thousands of cookies with "seconds" for
Neighboring children, draperies for a sanctuary, 48 years ironing "fair linens."
Peg keeps right on doing the jobs that need to be done.

Leading Girl Scouts for years, working with PTA and the League.
First Vestry woman at the old, historic church. A companion to Art
In his pioneering work for CW. Raising four children.
Now seven Grandchildren and six "greats", this close family gives her energy
To find new jobs that need to be done; Peg continues.

She's not much for fanfare. Not eager for center stage.
Her calm, steady manner undergirds all that she does.
A twinkle and smile show the place of fun in her everyday life.
She seems to bridge differences in generations as
Peg keeps doing the jobs that need to be done.

Peg Smith

She grew up in Rochester, New York. In 1951 Peg came to Williamsburg with her husband and four children. They lived in the Historic District of Colonial Williamsburg and Peg's activities revolved around CW, Bruton Parish Church and family.

Margaret (Peg) Brigham Smith
November 12, 1920 - February 23, 2006

I was the boy my father waited for. So far, there were all girls in the family. But he and I were very close. We collected stamps together and I had a workbench right beside his. He taught me patience, many skills and how to organize the job that needed to be done. It was a happy childhood and I planned to be a teacher. My parents were both very social, active in the church. I learned from them about giving to the community.

I met my future husband Art in 1940, and soon we were married in my hometown, Rochester, New York. We later lived in Ithaca, New York, for ten years and we had four children, two of each. We came to Williamsburg in 1951 when Art was appointed Audio Visual Director of Colonial Williamsburg (CW). Therefore, we were able to live in the historic area and what a wonderful place it was! Art made thirty some films, and we were all involved in the making of them. I just did whatever he needed — a "gopher" or anything else. He involved the children as well. I would never change anything about those thirty-two years on Francis Street. There are literally dozens of stories about what the children did growing up: such as, our son Tim climbing the Palace Wall to get inside and guide the visitors through the garden maze or just generally be helpful to them. Of course, he was supposed to be in school at that time!

A group of neighborhood children had a lemonade stand in front of the CW Prentis Shop for two summers. They were quite ingenious and would hop on the CW tour bus, ride to the nearby Woodlands Hotel, get ice from the machines, ride back and that way keep the drinks chilled all day long. Quite successful it was until CW closed them down. It was just like one big family when we lived in the historic area. Everyone knew each other and we all felt a responsibility of being representatives for CW, even the children. Little things like making sure that they put away their bicycles, for these bikes were not part of the eighteenth century scene. This helped them to be more responsible about other things as they grew up. It was wonderful for them and we all talk about those times when we get together.

As the children grew, I was involved in the Parent-Teacher Association, Girl Scouts and the church. My Girl Scout Troop began in the fourth grade and went through high school. I received the Thanks Badge, of which I am very proud as I think scouting teaches values and skills that are so important in today's world.

Bruton Parish Church became very much a part of my life. I was involved in the women's organization, the church bazaar and I am making jams and jellies now for their gift shop. Last year, it was about 607 jars. In 1969, I was elected to the Vestry, the first woman they had ever had. Then I served two more terms. One time, the sun-damaged draperies in the church needed to be replaced, but it was too expensive. I made the replacements myself - in about a month. Then I became a church guide (thirty years) and was made Altar Guild Chairman in 1966 and have continued until now (thirty-five years). The guild is one of the activities which has meant more to me than most anything else.

I was one of travel editor George Wright's "street walkers" taking surveys for CW by talking to the visitors on the street. I also made cookies for the Abby Aldrich Rockefeller Museum for their Christmas time festivities. At last count it was about 27,712. The neighborhood children really liked this time of year because I kept a "house basket" with all the slightly imperfect cookies. After school, they would all come to the back door looking for a handout!

When we first moved here, there was no League of Women Voters (I was active in the League in New York), so when a league was started in Williamsburg, I participated. I am active in the Williamsburg Garden Club; I get a lot of enjoyment from that. It has been a very happy life. Art and I were married 50 years and when he was sick before he died, the children and grandchildren were so supportive of me. We are a close family of four children, seven grandchildren and six great grandchildren.

As I look back, I can see how much influence that church and faith in God has had on me for my whole lifetime and was the source of strength and courage for everything that came along. When I was first struggling with some of life's problems I thought of the older neighbor lady who said, when I asked how I could repay her, "You can't pay back, but you can pass it on to someone else." That's a message I would share with younger people.

When I get up in the morning, I get out of bed quickly because I have things to do: for example, one Christmas I had two nephews who lost their father at a young age and I decided to make them family photo albums. I wanted them to know their family stories. My children got wind of this and also wanted their own stories. I ended up making eleven books as gifts for that year. I brought them up to that date and told them to continue from there.

My future projects include a genealogy of both my family and Art's (with the name "Smith," you know that is a complicated work) and tackling the stamp collection which hasn't been touched for years.

Nancy, artist, on the wings of an angel.

Her wings frame the door, like a mother hen enfolding her chicks.
The angel not only greets but defines the home space within.
Birdhouses and barns and cottages and ships.
Enclosures, safe resting places for the body and the soul.
The outside and inside are like paintings and sculptures.
It is studio and home to Nancy, the artist.

With clear, warm eyes she not only looks but sees
Those places not visited. Experiences of the imagination become a
Colorful canvas, a piece of carved wood, a painted panel.
Weddings and flowers and cakes with candles and
Angels, lots of angels. It is her spirit that must find expression.
Nancy, artist, on the wings of an angel.

Her very presence is color. All colors. Bubbling and flowing
Into art work. The energy and passion and joy
Shows through the simple figures and places and common things.
The purity of each piece stands solid. There is integrity, humility,
Fun, whimsy, expection, surprise.
Nancy, artist, on the wings of an angel.

Nancy Thomas

Living in Germany after World War II influenced her early childhood years. Returning to the US, Nancy lived in Richmond until marriage, then moved to Yorktown, VA, where her career in folk art was established.

Nancy Gardner Thomas
Born August 5, 1938

I'll tell you about my family first. My grandfather, a Baptist minister on my mother's side, died before I was born. My father was Chief of Labor Relations in occupied Berlin right after the war. We lived in Berlin for a year, when I was nine years old, until we were evacuated during the Berlin Airlift. My mother was a homemaker until age 40 when she went to work in Richmond. I had a younger brother with whom I was very close, and still am. In Germany, my brother and I were the only people that we had. Germany was in shambles when we arrived. The German government hadn't even cleared out all the bodies from the wreckage. We lived in a German duchess's house, and my brother and I would sit on the floor and make clay figures hour after hour, days on end. His would be cars with hoods that lifted and mine would be houses with all the furnishings. While there, I found out there was no Santa Claus, because there were only German toys, and my parents couldn't get anything from America. That period in my life made a lasting impression on me; I'm still painting about it.

After we went back home to Richmond, I took piano and dancing lessons and all those things that children did. I idolized all my teachers and wanted to be just like them. As far as mentors go, I just kind of figured it out for myself. At about age six, I began doing comic strips. My first characters were a head of lettuce and carrots and there was a storyline that went with them. I did thousands of them. I had a goal of doing five strips a day and would try to complete one adventure each day. Over the years, my age was reflected in cartoons such as "Millie the Model" which I did later on. These comics reflected my growing up. I also played with paper dolls; I would make doll clothes, furniture out of matchboxes, and all kinds of accessories to go with the dolls.

My great aunt Myrtle, a Baptist Missionary, was very important to me. She cared a lot about me. When I was about 13 or so, I really wanted a pair of red underpants. My mother said, "No, indeed." Nevertheless, in the mail came a package from my aunt with a pair of red pants. In her youth, my mother was somewhat of a rebel in that she would do things like sneaking out of her bedroom window, smoking with the girls, dancing ... things that Baptist daughters shouldn't do. The struggles I experienced with my mother (she would say "black" and I would say "white") who saw a bit of "the rebel" in me, like herself, were probably a factor in strengthening me. We weren't made to go to church, only if we wanted to, and we usually wanted to for social reasons. My growth was more spiritual than religious. I have always felt closeness to God and have been greatly influenced by Nature. I believe in angels; I believe that I have a guardian angel.

I was always an artist ... always painting or drawing. I can never remember a time when I wasn't doing some kind of art. I had to, I was driven. When my children were still quite young, I wanted some extra money and I did what I knew best. So I did pen and ink drawings and sold them to a shop in Virginia Beach where I was living at the time. My first check was for $7.00 for the whole lot of them. At that time I had been doing posters, decorating my rooms at home and was very surprised when my drawings sold. It really took off and a Virginia Beach woman wanted to represent me to a firm in New York. I received a letter from the firm saying "We're going to make someone big out of you..." I was in my late 20's and this New York situation scared me, so I stopped doing anything for about five years. I had been getting huge orders from shops, had to get the neighbor kids in to help me with framing, the artwork was taking over our house and I could see it becoming unmanageable. Success in art never entered my mind. I wasn't prepared for it.

The next stage of my life was a turning point for me. My mother became ill with Lou Gehrig's disease. I was in my early 30's and wanted to take care of her. My father died shortly after her diagnosis, and I think that he just couldn't face living life without her, so he died. My husband supported me in keeping her at home until she had to go to Riverside Hospital for two months before she died. I started working at Riverside as a secretary because of needing money for her care; it was expensive. But I knew what I had to do. After she died, I felt that I needed to paint. I had looked at mortality, my own, and I had to do this. It was very compelling and powerful. I said "Show me the way and I'll do it." I realized that this was a gift that I had and must do something with it. I tried to get into galleries around here, the Yorktown-Williamsburg area; for example, the Peninsula of Fine Arts (PFA), Yorktown Art Association, The Twentieth Century Gallery, etc., and no one was interested. Folk art just wasn't around; no one was doing this.

However, Shirley Ferguson, at PFA, found one of my paintings in their closet and recognized it as something unique. She gave a party for me, and because she was well connected, that was my introduction to the art world. I had the time to do art because my pharmacist husband worked long hours and different schedules. I often used our children as models, and I just painted and painted.

The Mary Emmerling connection is another one of those mysterious happenings that just did happen. Mary Emmerling, an author, art collector, and now editor, had a major influence on my life. It was at the time (1981 or so) that Early American Country was getting a bit old and tired. I saw a picture of Mary Emmerling combining modern with country art and contacted her. My husband and I drove through the night to New York with 40 of my pieces in our pickup truck. Mary bought everything except one carved fish. I always wondered why Mary didn't buy the fish. Later she told me that she didn't buy it because she didn't want it to go to my head! She opened her new shop with all my pieces featured. Martha Stewart, a new caterer then, even did the opening. From there, it just went on and on — decorating the White House tree for President and Mrs. Reagan, the movie producers of Tootsie leasing every piece of work in Mary Emmerling's New York shop for the film, commissions coming from Virginia Governor Baliles; it was a very "heady time." I found a place to rent across from On The Hill in Yorktown, pouring all the money I made back into the business, so I didn't have much for rent. I would sit in this little place, paint and sing "Band of angels comin' after me..." and my husband asked me why I didn't open the door, so people can come in to see my work. I did that, and they came.

The subjects of my painting often reflect many things, which I can't do or be ... so I paint them. For example, I'm not a big gardener so I paint flowers. I never had a wedding, we eloped, so I love to paint weddings. There are so many things that I paint from my head ... I think about Emily Dickinson and her writings and she hardly ever left home. It is extraordinary where the mind can take you and amazing what people are capable of doing.

Business is the most difficult obstacle I have to handle. There are men and women working for me supporting their families on my artwork. I feel this responsibility. It's a curse as well as a privilege. This is something that has been put in my path, one of the things I have learned from. For example, men in our culture have had the primary responsibility of supporting the family. I had to start thinking the way a man does and, suddenly, I have a greater appreciation for the role of men. I have learned so much about all people.

I'm basically a "homebody." I need a home base and it's comfortable for me here. Our family came to Yorktown when living in Newport News and found a place while driving around Yorktown where I have lived now for 33 years. I remember seeing a woman then with a bandana on her head riding a bicycle with a wicker basket. The other day I was thinking that here I am riding a bicycle with a wicker basket and a bandana on my head....

Living in the Williamsburg-Yorktown area, I am free of competition. Living here has been a privilege, and I can be myself and my work is my own, not affected by needing to compete with thousands of other artists ... such as in New York.

I would tell younger women: "Follow your passion, and you will be successful. Listen to yourself and ask questions like, 'What gives me energy? Where is my spirit?' Then you will have a successful life." I was fortunate because it has always been clear to me that artwork is what I must do.

My next project is to get the business part of my life figured out. I will continue to do artwork all the time and, perhaps, in my eighties I will feel as though I have mastery in the field of art in which I work.

Sufficient unto Herself. Madelynn

Her tiny frame fits into the covered rocker like a hand into a glove.
Arms hugging the knees, she's comfortable within herself and with others.
The fine, light colored hair is collected naturally for ease of care, work.
Eyes connecting easily, with kindness, to the visitor. She is what she is.
Sufficient unto herself.

Madelynn warmly gestures toward the photo gallery under glass on her table
In order to share the interesting lives of five children and 10 "grands."
Sprinkled throughout her efficient apartment are reminders of her life.
Nursing, teaching, mothering, managing a restaurant, football, music, plays.
Sufficient unto herself.

On the table are cuttings of a purple plant taking root under her care and
A book listing visitors to the College gardens, where she works every day.
Plants and seeds are like good friends to her. The whole earth is her concern.
Her strong, suntanned hands gesture easily as she talks with modesty.
Sufficient unto herself.

Professors and presidents, students and travelers. There are few
Boundaries to where she has touched people with her seeds and wisdom.
Family is first, even though they are spread far to the East and West.
With enthusiasm, she plans her visits and trips as carefully as her gardens.
Sufficient unto herself.

Her vision of the future is positive as she does what she has been doing for
Years, with the goal of doing more, including a plan
To make a quilt for each child and grandchild as did grandmothers of yore.
With humor, practicality and common sense, she continues to be
Sufficient unto herself.

Madelynn Watkinson

She was mother of many children, cared for an ailing husband and ran a restaurant. Now in Williamsburg, Madelynn spends nearly every day tending the William and Mary Gardens near Merchant's Square, sharing her knowledge with all who come.

Madelynn Ann Whitehead Watkinson
Born September 26, 1924

My family lived in Hartford, Connecticut and my grandparents lived in East Haddan, Connecticut where I spent the summers. I was pretty much of a tomboy and liked playing baseball and going swimming. We had coaches who were mentors to all of us swimmers. I was eleven by that time. My family was strongly behind me. My father, along with other school parents, hired an Olympic coach for training practice. We practiced three times a week, but because of the war, the Olympics was cancelled. My father had a good position and after I started school, my mother became a buyer in a department store. I went to a public school, then a Catholic nursing school. Then I entered the Nurses Cadet Corps in 1943. When I was through theory (training), you went into the Corps and they sent you wherever they wanted to. Everything was hurried up during the war to get people prepared to handle jobs that were needed. After that, I got married and had five kids.

My greatest accomplishment was having five kids. My husband and I had three children close together, then a space between the next two, like two different sets. It was funny, when the three oldest, who were in college, were coming home, the youngest one told his teacher in school that "company's coming."

Turning points in my early life came so quickly because the war came so fast. There wasn't a time for "youth"; we lost that time in our lives. Friends from childhood were gone. Who knew that half of your class wouldn't come home from the war? We kept sorrow inside because we weren't encouraged to talk about it. As a nurse I worked with wounded soldiers when they came back; I was with a team of orthopedic specialists. A real turning point in my life was when I took courses at Yale University. I lived close to Yale and took the classes because I wanted to learn more. I studied business law, volume feeding, and all kinds of things. When I was pregnant with our fourth, I went to work in a restaurant in East Haddam. I was hired to become a waitress, as an apprentice, and the following year I became manager of the Goodspeed Restaurant and soon became the caterer to its Opera House.

I didn't have big obstacles, except for going to meetings in the restaurant management field, and I was the only woman. I found cigars and cognac with an abbreviated version of my name "M.W." on them. The men assumed that I was a male, too (I was the only female participant), and I was surrounded by men at the meetings. But I try not to let things become obstacles.

Eventually, my husband became ill, but he remained at home. He wasn't bedridden but was cared for three-and-a-half years before he died. At this time, the two youngest children were at home, so they were a help too.

I came to live in Williamsburg when I turned 65. My daughter and son-in-law planned to have children and wanted a grandmother around.

I volunteered for different jobs in the town. I was weeding Adams Garden at the College of William and Mary when I got two tickets for parking. My daughter told me to go to the Facilities and Management Department where I first met Roy Williams, the manager of the grounds. He told me that the garden "was mine," and gave me an official parking pass. I began a list of volunteers and even got a greenhouse. The students who were assigned to do community service for some infringement of the college rules were assigned to work with me. That was okay with me. I averaged seven days a week, six hours a day working in the gardens. I like brilliant colors that attract butterflies and hummingbirds. I've kept records so that someone else will know what to do in the future. Roy always stood behind me when I needed something for the garden. When Tim Sullivan became president of the college, a Horticultural Manager was needed and hired. I also go digging with Gerry Johnson, a geologist, from the college. I've taken his classes for four years with the idea that if I could do the fieldwork, others could do it too. One of my favorite keepsakes, which is now owned by the college, is a nine million-year-old shell from a whale that was sent to the Smithsonian; I helped dig it up.

I really enjoy what I do — that's one of the keys to success. I enjoy reading, sewing, making quilts, cooking and listening to the singing group, "Chicago," when I take a bath (smile). I want to make quilts for all the children and grandchildren and have already collected the materials. I'm also interested in environmental issues; it's hard not to be interested when you've spent years digging in the earth like I have.

I tell young women, "Anybody, really, can do it! Things are such now that women can plan to do whatever they want. You have choices: You may stay at home and teach manners and common sense for the first few years and then go out and do whatever you want. Having children does not mean having a 'handicap.' You have to work hard, but you can do it. It was harder when I was working, but still I did it."

I'm continuing to do what I can for my community. For example, I attended meetings to save the hospital and drug store. I think it's important to give back to a community that's been good to you and Williamsburg has. I just keep on doing what needs to be done.

Two Millies

She graciously serves coffee, moves about with poise and warmth.
It is easy to picture international celebrities in this place
Filled with lovely antiques.
Richmond Hill is home to Millie.

She lights up when talking about gardens and
Bubbles right over showing her well equipped kitchen and folk art.
She gives personality to this home where significant funds were raised with
Commitment, sincerity and fun. This is Millie.

Across the street, upstairs to the right, an office is
Packed full of pictures and certificates and emblems and posters and rackets
And books and boxes and one large tennis ball in the center of the desk.
This space belongs to a beloved coach, teacher, mentor. This is Millie.

The large window shows an entire court below. Upstairs, the Museum
Surrounds her with what has been a lifetime of energy, passion, and skill.
Her small, compact body easily shifts from hostess to sportswoman.
A rare mixture of strength, beauty, drive, sensitivity...this is Millie.

Millie West

An enthusiastic athlete, she became a faculty member of the College of William and Mary in the Women's Athletic Department. Millie is also a gardener, recognized fund raiser and community servant.

Millie Barrett West
Born October 26, 1934

I grew up in Cedartown, Georgia with two older sisters in a close knit family. Our family had very modest resources but my parents did a lot with what we had. My parents sacrificed so that we could have opportunities they never had. My father spent any extra time he had outdoors. He loved hunting, fishing and being athletic with me. Mother was more interested in making a home for the family, being active in the church and being involved in music. Both of my parents were smart in spite of the fact that they lacked the advantage of a formal education. This made them determined that their three daughters would have that opportunity.

I was small and precocious and would try just about anything. I played all sports but, like my father, I was self-taught in all of them. Swimming and tennis were always my favorites, those were the "summer" sports, but basketball dominated the scene during the school year. That was the only organized sport for girls in school. My father constructed a full basketball court in our yard so that my friends and I could practice a real game situation.

Our family activities were centered on the church. I belonged to all the organizations offered for young people by the church, the community and the schools. That included taking piano and voice lessons, singing in the church choir, playing clarinet in the school band, playing parts in the school plays, singing in the high school glee club and playing as many sports as possible.

My family was very supportive of whatever I was doing, but as I began to focus on sports as a career, they tried to influence me to embrace a more "substantial" career. Not to be deterred, I attended Georgia State College for Women (now Georgia College) on a work-study program throughout my four years and majored in Health and Physical Education. I also worked each summer to help defray the cost of undergraduate and graduate education.

At graduation, I was offered a graduate assistantship in Health and Physical Education at the University of Maryland. A professor, who had been like a mother to me, thought I should get a graduate degree and encouraged me to accept the assistantship. My mother was reluctant to give it her blessing so my professor, Grace Chapin, drove mother and me to Washington so we could look over the situation. I accepted the offer and enrolled in the Master's program. My second year at Maryland, I served as an Acting Assistant Professor filling in for a professor on leave of absence. My thesis was a research project on Motor Learning. That study on Motor Learning was among the early studies in this field and was published; for many years it was a resource for those studying Motor Learning.

I graduated in 1959 and came to the College of William and Mary (W&M) for my first "real" job as an instructor of tennis and swimming. Different from today, instructors were not encouraged to continue their graduate work or research projects; the main emphasis was teaching and coaching. W&M had more athletic programs for women than most colleges during this era; the teams had short schedules and were as much a social function, as they were a competitive game. It was customary for the teams to enjoy tea and cookies together after the game or match. Try to image that today!

The men's and women's physical education and athletic programs were housed in separate departments. This ended in 1986. There were minimal funds available for women's teams in those days, and a coach did whatever was necessary to field a team. We taught, coached, transported, raised money and traveled with the team housing them in dorms and with friends; we helped each other with the teams. Teams were born out of student interest, not as a mandate for equality. It was in 1968 that I became Chairman of the Physical Education Department, which also included Women's Athletics and Intramurals.

I met my husband, Marvin, toward the end of my first year at W&M. Marvin received his undergraduate degree from W&M and a Doctor of Dentistry Degree from the Medical College of Virginia. He returned to Williamsburg to practice and had completed a year of practice by the time we met. We were married in 1966 and have been happily rooted in Williamsburg all these years. Marvin has always been supportive of my activities; however, he has never totally adapted to my schedule. He commented on many occasions, "If you wouldn't try to play tennis with one hand and cook with the other." (In other words, why do you insist on doing so many things at one time?)

The women's swimming team was one I initiated in 1965 to accommodate the many women enrolling at the college with strong swimming backgrounds and a desire to continue to swim competitively. They were excellent swimmers and went on to a 50-1 record over five years. Teaching and coaching in an informal setting and traveling extensively with students produces meaningful relationships that continue well beyond the college years. These relationships are the reward for me as coach and teacher.

The single most important happening for women's athletics was the passing of the Education amendment Act of 1972, better known as Title IX. The regulations governing this law were finally published in 1976. The regulations mandated equitable athletic programs for men and women. As the chairman of the department, I was fully aware of funding inequities throughout the program but had been able to make some advances but none of them significant. Therefore, armed with Title IX at my side, I started the crusade for better funding for women on campus. I took on an aggressive and often unpopular role in an effort to create more opportunities for women and to improve their athletic experience at W&M. This was the beginning of a drive that made a difference for women, and it continues to do so under the leaders following me. The Women's Athletic Program at W&M today is of the highest caliber.

Another significant happening for women's athletics was when the Wightman Cup Tournament was brought to W&M in 1983. This is a women's professional tennis match between players from the U.S. and Great Britain, which began in 1923 by Hazel Wightman. After some negotiations, I became the tournament chairman and women's athletics became one of the beneficiaries of the tournament. This was a huge undertaking, but at the same time it provided the first major opportunity to raise funds for women's athletics. As a result of its success, the first endowment for women's athletics was established. The Wightman is dormant at this time primarily due to the overwhelming strength of the U.S. Team. Efforts were made to transform it into the Ryder Cup format, but the United States Tennis Association (USTA) decided, instead, to put more emphasis on the FED Cup, which is the women's counterpart to the Davis Cup.

The men and women's tennis programs are among the oldest programs at W&M and since my arrival at the college, this has been a passion of mine. Facilities and scholarships have been a prime concern to me. Team schedules expanded include the full school term and this led to the need to have access to indoor practice space during the winter and inclement weather. The closest indoor facility was in Newport News, (Virginia), which required at least an hour and a half of travel daily. Add this time to a two-hour practice and you lose an enormous amount of study time. It was clear that an indoor facility on campus was needed. Mark McCormack, a strong supporter of tennis, committed funds to build the state-of-the-art McCormack-Nagelsen indoor tennis facility that we enjoy today. It sounds easy now, but it took years of work planning to make this facility a reality. I could have easily given up along the way, but I was obsessed with determination to complete this dream. I feel sure that my perseverance and determination came from my mother who experienced major losses as a child. (She came home from school to find their house burned to the ground, and her mother died when she was ten, so she had to drop out of school to take care of her four younger brothers and sisters.) She did what she had to do then, and she continued to do that throughout her life. Directly and indirectly, she taught me that I could do anything I put my mind to.

Founding the Tennis Hall of Fame at W&M in 1995 was another project, which required a lot of planning and research as well as major fund raising. (This is still the case each year as national pioneers and tennis players are inducted and the exhibit is expanded.) The Tennis Hall of Fame is located on the second floor, and it is housed in the beautiful McCormack-Nagelsen Tennis Center. This is the only women's tennis hall of fame in the country, and it's a jewel for W&M and a tremendous asset for our tennis programs.

The college has given me so much and so many opportunities that I would never have had otherwise, and it has been a privilege to spend my entire career here. For certain, I received much more than I've given. Much of this would not have been possible without the support of my husband Marvin and my friends. As a professional in Williamsburg and an active participant in the W&M Alumni Association, Marvin helped expand my involvement beyond my immediate circle of work at the college. He is my reality check!

My advice to young people is: "Don't be a taker. Give back more than you are given. Be passionate about things you believe in, and if you think it's important, never give up. With a little luck, knowledge, and a lot of perseverance, you will accomplish much more than you ever thought you could."

In my retirement, I'm still Director of Special Projects at the College, Curator of the Women's Tennis Hall of Fame and serve on several boards. Currently, some of those are the Williamsburg Community Health Foundation, the Old Point National Bank Advisory Board, the Virginia Sports Hall of Fame, the USTA FED Cup and the Williamsburg Garden Club Executive Board. Recently I was asked to serve as an advisor to the Dean of the Business School! Yes, I accepted!

Joy Brady

Shades of copper, orange and peach.
Arms curved open to embrace all.
Laughter, humor, reaching out.
Loving, caring, and giving,
Larger than Life ...

Joy!

Joy Lunsford Brady

Joy Lunsford Brady
October 6, 1940-February 10, 2006
Written by her husband Donald Brady

Joy was raised in Detroit by her parents, Agnes (Jonnie) and William (Red), and her older sister, Carol. Her father came to Detroit from Georgia at 16 years of age looking for work in the General Motors (GM) factories. GM said he looked like he was 18, and he was hired. He worked for 44-plus years at Chevrolet Gear and Axle. Her mother taught in a one-room schoolhouse in Georgia before coming to Detroit to marry her father. She was a stay-at-home mom, as was the norm then.

Joy attended Detroit public schools. She went to Cooley High School and graduated in June 1958. One of her most vivid memories was taking four years of Latin; she would get up every morning at 5 a.m. so her mother could drill her on the Latin homework for that day. Joy's mother was her first real mentor because she had a passion for reading and education in general. As a result, Joy was such a good reader in grade school that she would read to the kids during lunch hour. Many years later as a retired teacher in Williamsburg, she read to a group of preschoolers at story time sponsored by Barnes and Noble Book Store in the character of Mrs. Wainright, who always wore a large and decorated hat. The children and their parents just "ate this up."

She attended Detroit Institute of Technology (DIT) and then transferred to Wayne State University where she received her bachelor's degree. She then taught English at Mackenzie High School. Joy later obtained her master's degree in English Liberal Arts. Her goal was to become an excellent English teacher and educator and she succeeded as her teacher reviews were always in the superior range. While working toward her master's degree her thesis advisers Dr. Patricia Hernlund and Dr. Ellen Brown became her mentors. They sharpened her writing skills and required her to think and write in a more exact way.

Joy had several achievements of which she was very proud, because each had its own set of challenges:
1. She taught 31 years in the Detroit Public School system, basically all-black inner-city schools. She loved teaching and loved the kids, and was thrilled to see the scholastic growth in them. Her patience was really tested when kids showed up with no desire to learn.
2. Completing the work on her master's degree as it took her several years. Her graduate work was extremely difficult because, after teaching all day, she was challenged at a high level in the evening.
3. Joy was diagnosed with breast cancer in June 1988, and was an 18-year cancer survivor when she died. More importantly, she helped so many people who had cancer and other medical problems by showing them how to deal with these challenges.

4. Co-authoring CONVERSATIONS WITH REMARKABLE WOMEN with Sandy Lenthall was a labor of love. We had moved to Williamsburg, Virginia, in January 1999. Joy and Sandy met through a mutual friend, and they talked about some of incredible backgrounds of their neighbors. She never expected to help write a book in retirement.

Joy and I met at DIT. We were married October 19, 1963. We came from different religious dominations, but both agreed that whatever we did, we would do it together. This was a real challenge, as both families were unhappy at first, and we got married in a bridge church. We had no children, but were blessed with a lot of nieces and nephews. Our marriage of 42-plus years was very close as best friends, lovers, and just caring life-partners. We helped each other succeed by helping each other. Yes, both of us knew we were blessed in our marriage.

Mackenzie High School had over 3,000 students and over 150 teachers. The different departments were very close as they dealt with the same students in previous semesters (they would advise each other how to get through to that student). Joy learned, early on, that one should teach to the students that were there to learn; her message to the ones that weren't interested — flunk in silence. She had several techniques for controlling a classroom: she was always on her feet, she had her student cards with their phone numbers on her desk, and instead of calling the students' names she would read off their phone number (a big attention getter), and if a student was really acting up she would get nose to nose with him or her. Only on a rare occasion would she have to send a student to the counselor.

Early in Joy's teaching career, she had a very bad day at school when a student was murdered. A gang member had been pushing a small student around, turning his tray over in the lunchroom, etc., and after several other incidents like that the young man had had enough. The next day the young man asked the gang member to go outside and he shot the gang member six times. It was winter, and the blood all over the snow quickly made her think about what some of these students face daily. This horrible event was something she never forgot.

Joy had a kit car (a London Roadster convertible – made to resemble a 1949 MG TD Series), a little two-seater that you couldn't lock. The parking lot was at the side of the school with a big chain link fence separating the athletic field from the parking lot. A teacher friend had her car stolen one day, and the next day she drove her husband's car and it too was stolen (he was a Detroit police detective). When Joy was teaching on the first floor, a number of teachers would come by to check on their cars hourly, although about 30 cars were stolen a year, Joy's car was never touched!

The highest compliment was when former students would come and seek her out to thank her for helping change their lives. They went to college, entered the work force and the military, and how proud they were at what they had accomplished. She had an honor student who had gone to Harvard, and because she had taught him the basics so well, he was doing well and told her that many in his classes did not have his solid preparation.

Also, Joy taught Speech at Wayne State University, at night, for about five years – all students were required to take a basic speech course. One of her students was in Spain making a presentation, and the airline lost all his audio-visual equipment. He then wrote all he could remember about the basics of giving a good speech. He said it was one the best presentations he ever gave.

Joy did see the world change, and it distressed her to see the lack of respect for authority and education: parents couldn't control their children as they had no structure in their lives. Education was devalued because discipline problems were not dealt with. The Church no longer had the important role that it used to just a generation prior. You now have grandparents raising their children's children. She always felt education was the key. It gave kids a sense of self worth to think they had a future, and could make a positive contribution in the world.

If Joy had been asked "what advice would you give to young women today?" I'm quite sure her answer would be something like this. "You need to respect yourself, be proud of who you are, and get a good education. Education is never wasted. You can use it for your own success, pass this learning on to your own children or others and more importantly, it gives you power, energy and strength to tackle almost anything." Joy believed that "if you can read you can cook."

Further, she understood that there is a Supreme Being and you are responsible for using the talents that God gave you. The Ten Commandments and the Golden Rule were never out-of-date.

Joy was a spiritual person with life experiences. She helped a number of people by her advice, sympathy, and new ideas and planning many fun things. In Detroit she read the newspaper for the blind on the radio (only the blind had special receivers to hear the broadcast). She started and taught mystery courses to senior citizens at the Birmingham Area Senior Coordinating Council (BASCC). This was a summer program. They called themselves the Senior Super Sleuths. They read and discussed mystery stories; they met a number of local authors and took field trips with the authors. At her church, she took over an evening circle that was dying and energized it by bringing in women to speak on current women's issues; as a result, it became very well attended.

Joy was remarkable because her presence could light up a room. It was her enthusiasm and zest for life, showing in her interest in others. She was a connector; she was so good at this – several of her connections even got married. She wanted to share her friends with others and it was this caring that made her so special. Her legacy is one of wanting to help others and sharing her love for others. She never met a stranger. Surely, hers was a life well lived.

Tribute to Joy

I remembered Joy Brady often, after she and Don moved to Williamsburg. Of course I did: she was not a person you could forget. Her enthusiasm and boundless energy resulted in a larger-than-life personality which radiated through every room she ever entered.

I don't remember her ever backing down on a worthwhile endeavor, for giving up was not in her philosophy. In her teaching, Joy insisted year after year in upholding standards and in devoting herself to convincing high school students to love literature as much as she did. My group of friends learned about this from her, but we thoroughly believed it. I remember marveling that "her kids" seemed to love Shakespeare, love all of American literature, and even (sometimes) love writing. Much of that was her love - reaching them because of her extraordinary charisma.

Another one of her teaching endeavors was with the opposite age group at the Birmingham, Michigan Senior Center, where she drew large crowds to her mystery reading group. That was when I really got to know her. Later I was one of her advisors, with Dr. Ellen Brown, for her master's thesis. It isn't every master's student who becomes a lasting friend of her advisors. Her thesis was excellent: intelligent, illuminating, and well researched. But that doesn't explain why she and I and Ellen kept going to events and meeting for lunch, going to the Stratford Festival, and generally settling into a friendship that centered around her vibrant love of life and seeing and doing new things with friends. She savored life so much that it was impossible to be a stick-in-the-mud around her.

The tragedy of her cancer struck all of her friends, too. It was long enough ago so that the disease, the treatment and the chances of survival were all virtually unknown. She threw herself into the battle as she did everything - with her whole heart. Somehow, the wonderful marriage between Joy and Don not only survived the cancer but also strengthened their bond.

As Joy's parents aged, she used the lessons she had learned from her cancer battle to help them cope and buoy them up. Both the Bradys were amazing in their resourcefulness and perseverance in helping Joy's parents go through the trials of their long decline.

The Bradys always went to church, but not just for weekly services. It was a very important part of their every day to participate fully in their spiritual life.

And all this was done with a happy heart. I remember Joy entering a room like a force of nature, a red-haired whirlwind of energy, smiling broadly, and speaking immediately and urgently about a new, exciting idea or project, or simply about how good it was to see friends again. The room was changed by her presence; we were changed by her exuberant embrace of life.

By Dr. Patricia Hernlund
Professor Emeritus, Wayne State University

Small in Stature, Tall in Accomplishments.

Large, fashionable sunglasses dominated her small face
When she arrived at the door after driving from Virginia Beach on July 3rd.
At 88 years, she continues to be determined, and "gets on and does it."
Small, strong and adventurous.

Whether it be the Green Berets, traveling with Aunt Anna, saving the dolphins,
Painting in the Algerian desert, visiting her Chinese "daughter" in Hong Kong,
Giving a talk about her novel at the library, being photographer in Germany, she is
Small, strong and adventurous.

Her soft white hair frames an expression breaking into frequent smiles.
Eyes that twinkle with enthusiasm and delight catch attention.
Her hands move carefully and purposefully to accentuate whatever the topic becomes.
Doris is full of life, determined, creative and adventurous.

Doris Caroline Baker

Doris Caroline Baker

Born September 25, 1917

I've been so lucky in life and have had such a lot of fun!

My great grandfather, a surveyor, chose farmland near a group of settlers as his home, which later became the village of Bancroft, Michigan. His daughter married and she and her husband inherited the farm. Her husband died when my father was only two years old; however, the land was productive and my father was able to graduate with a degree in forestry and then, together with my mother, went to Montana and worked in the U.S. Forest Service. Unfortunately, the Great Depression began about the same time my father left the forest service to help his mother take care of the family farm in Michigan. So, I grew up there on the farm during a tough economic time but had the advantage of learning early many valuable lessons. Lessons such as not to waste things, that you must work hard and you don't get something for nothing. I remember one Christmas in particular when I was eight years old. My grandma, mother, daddy and I exchanged names for twenty-five-cent presents. I was the only one who got a present that cost a dollar. It was a green and orange scarf that I had to pretend to like. They were so happy to give it to me. I guess if the Great Depression did anything good, it showed that loving friends and family are more important than money. In our small community everyone helped their neighbors and depended upon each other for all kinds of assistance.

Daddy was so handsome and gentle, mother was out-going and ambitious for me, and grandma was there whenever I needed her. All my family read books, loved animals and nature, and told me stories of past adventures. I had chores to do but I also had (what I believe is critical for all children) time to dream. Also, there was never a question that I would have a college education. I grew up knowing this. Not a bad combination for any child!

During my high school years, I was sure I would have a career as an artist. Eventually, it became clear I would need to learn something else in order to earn a living. To insure this I chose to major in education. Family economics required that I work my way through college so off I went to Eastern Michigan State with one suit (which was entirely too heavy even for fall weather). I had two other dresses, which had been made out of several adult frocks and put together to fit me. I worked in a boarding house in which ten of us lived together sharing a small dormitory style bedroom, sleeping on cots in an unheated upstairs. Our chores included serving meals, cleaning and kitchen duties. We didn't know any better and thought that we were supposed to be happy. So we were. The women with whom I lived then have continued to be my close friends all these years.

When I was a junior, my father, who had just found a very lucrative job, died very suddenly in Chicago. Fortunately, my mother was with him. I just barely made it to graduation and got my first teaching job at $1200/year, which, at the time, was quite a good salary. My mother and I survived on that for seven years. In spite of shaky finances, mother insisted I spend a summer at Cranbrook Academy of Art, a place where world-famous artists lived and worked. It was wonderful! And, in spite of our lack of money, we went on a car trip to the west coast so I could see the places I'd heard so much about.

Seven years after my father's death, my mother died. I continued teaching first and second grades four more years. Then, three little words, "Adventure for Teachers", an ad in the local newspaper, took me overseas to teach in a Department of Defense (DOD) school in Bad Tolz, Germany. It was a stroke of good fortune that led to many important changes in my life. That military base happened to be the first overseas assignment for the first group of U.S.Special Forces. Without any knowledge of the German language or American army personnel, and without the slightest experience or training in school administration, I became principal of the school. I credit my early life with its necessities for work and my family's encouragement and belief in me for the fact I was able to adapt to these changes and meet the challenges. At the same time, I was given the opportunity to travel all over Europe and also to China during a very pivotal time after World War II when cultures began to change dramatically. My family had stimulated a love of travel and an immense curiosity in me and I was finally able to paint and write and photograph to my heart's content, as they had hoped.

As a result of my friendship with the U.S. Special Forces (named "Green Berets" by President John F. Kennedy), I wrote a novel about them in 2002: *THE ORIGINALS*. A book called, *I'LL LET YOU KNOW WHEN WE GET THERE*, vignettes of my travels, will be coming.

Then, there was the little girl I "adopted" in Hong Kong. She was about nine years old when I began sending financial help as a foster parent. After visiting, I learned that the entire family lived on the monthly stipend. I visited her twice and also brought her to this country to visit. She now has two little girls and we are still in communication.

I came to Williamsburg after leaving the DOD school system in Europe and in retirement, I have found kindred spirits and mentors and an adopted family. Activities with friends made in writing and art groups as well as animal causes have kept me busy and happy.

What would I say to young women today? Just about everything has been accelerated to the point that there is practically no time for creative wondering. Whatever our talents or opportunity (luck), the world has a need for us. We just have to persist, reach out and find what we are meant to do.

Mary Gonzales

She is tall and plays at the piano with ease, with grace.
The lid is covered with framed pictures of family.
This is Mary Gonzales, family and music.

Silvery white hair scoops gently about her face.
It's a strong face, one that reflects prairie nurture and wisdom.
Elegant in her dress but straight forward in her manner
She combines rural simplicity,
Worldly experience and living life fully.
Mary is a woman of strength, classic beauty, warmth, and charm.

Mary Gonzales

Mary Gonzales
Born March 26, 1917

I was born and grew up in Elmwood, Nebraska. My mother was most influential as she was my piano teacher, which began at about age three or four years. She was the piano teacher for all the children in town. Elmwood had about 450 people when every one was at home and was about 24 miles from Lincoln.

There was a lot of music in this town: an orchestra, music programs in the schools and band concerts every weekend at the bandstand in the center of town. It really was due to the efforts of my mother and a few others that in this small prairie town there was so much emphasis upon music - and such good music. I don't know where my mother's music ability came from. My grandfather had a drug store in town and lived in the back of the store. In fact, my mother was born in that store and grew up there. My father had grown up on a farm that his father had homesteaded.

My father was very supportive of mother's efforts and I studied classical music in town until about age 12 when I went by train to the University of Nebraska School of Music in Lincoln and took organ lessons. My youngest sister also plays the organ. I have two sisters and one brother.

At the University, my cousin studied voice. She knew of my ability and suggested that I go to the Voice Studio at the Conservatory to see Madam Gutzmer. I knocked on the door and when she answered, I said, "my cousin suggested that I come." Madam responded, "I need an accompanist now." So I sat down and played the music she had, (my mother had taught me to sight read) and from then on I worked with her.

I attended the University of Nebraska Conservatory of Music but quit in order to marry my high school sweetheart. Don had moved to Washington, DC and gotten a job with the United Press as a journalist. He wrote to me saying, "I have a job. Come to DC and we'll get married." So I left on the midnight train in the middle of a blizzard, stopped in Chicago for a few days to visit relatives, then went on to Silver Springs, Maryland. We had a small, beautiful wedding, which was preceded by what turned out to be an organ concert because, when I was asked what music I wanted, I gave a very long list. It was just beautiful. In the early days of our marriage, I studied organ and practiced at the church where we were married.

I remember the Sunday night of Pearl Harbor vividly. The next morning Don had to report for duty and was activated. He had been in ROTC and commissioned as an officer at the University of Nebraska. He had always wanted to fly and was able to transfer from Field Artillery to the Army Air Corps where he learned to fly and then spent several years teaching other men how to fly. I became a "camp follower" and, eventually, we went to live in Dotham, Alabama where I continued with music by playing for the troops at the USO functions. We had a daughter while we were stationed there. From the time of her birth, we were told that she had a heart defect. In fact, the pediatrician counseled me that we would be unlikely to "keep her." I recall that at that time when the three of us were living in a small room in a rat-infested house near the military base, I was filled with such despair I couldn't see how I could possibly manage. It was a strong faith in God that helped me through this very difficult time. And, as always, it was in family and music in which I could also find strength. Then we moved back to Washington, DC where Don returned to his job with United Press. He began covering the White House and the State Department so he was very busy. This was during the Eisenhower Administration.

How did we get to Williamsburg? Well, Don met Carl Humelsine while he was covering the State Department and Carl was an Under Secretary of State. While waiting for the Secretary of State to appear for press conferences or meetings, the two men talked about their mutual interest and appreciation of old furniture. Then Carl was made the President of Colonial Williamsburg. Don had been thinking about making a change when Carl called inviting him to come to Williamsburg and look around. Then they would talk.

Donald did take the job offered in public relations for Colonial Williamsburg. At the beginning, we lived in the Blue Bell Tavern, which had a lovely basement apartment. There was a huge family room with carpeting and a fireplace and all of the basics in the lower level called the English basement. This area included a kitchen and when my husband's mother would come from Nebraska, she would do all of her baking in this kitchen. Our son, John, credits his grandmother and experiences with her in the kitchen, as that which encouraged him to eventually go to the Culinary Institute of America. He now has a restaurant and school in town.

When we came to Colonial Williamsburg in 1958, there were many activities for women such as garden clubs but there were fewer organizations involving music. Don's job required a lot of entertaining which I enjoyed thoroughly. In addition, I was asked by the national president of Delta Omicron to help establish a chapter of the music sorority at the College of William and Mary. This involved me with the students and created a great deal of the activity which took place in our home. In fact, the students would come over and study in one of the bedrooms upstairs, practice on the piano, and join us for meals. Also, their initiations were always held in our home. Between Colonial Williamsburg entertaining and my activities with the students and our active family life, we had a busy house at all times.

I was very busy but I love people. Life is always a challenge and it is wonderful especially if you enjoy and love people.

Jock Darling, organist at Bruton Parish Church, called me to help plan a series of concerts at Phi Beta Kappa Hall. Through activities with him and others in the community, we began the Wednesday Morning Music Club, which continues today. At first, this small group of people met at Jock and Mary Lee's home. Now, it has become a vibrant organization of many different people and activities.

Years ago, Don was invited to speak to a group in Traverse City, Michigan and I went along. After several summers of travel there, we decided to purchase a place and spent about two months there each summer. I continue to spend time in the summer there at Interlochen, Michigan.

I play all kinds of music but I guess it's "pop" music which I like the best. But then again, I really do like all kinds of music. Our community has so many musical offerings now and it is growing all the time.

What do I have to say to young women? Love one another. That is what this life is all about. I have had many experiences and have met many, many interesting people. My family means everything to me. (It might be of interest that the baby daughter with a serious heart defect is now 60 years old. Her heart still has an unusual beat.)

Yes, it really is all about loving one another.

Connie Lee, First Generation American

Trim and compact. Brown hairstyle short and easy.
She sits comfortably in jeans and sweater. No pretenses.
Her home is open, inviting the out of doors inside.
She is open and invites the stranger to come in also.

Surrounded by family treasures, comfortable places to have conversation.
Connie speaks quietly but with strength, credibility.
Her brown eyes laugh, then shadow and show the emotional range of
the conversation.
Humility and gratitude pepper her thoughts liberally, compassion abounds.
Her accomplishments blend into the activities of many and for many.
She is daughter, wife, mother and because of her daughter, activist.

Connie Lee is the first generation born of German parents
And she is grateful.

Connie Lee

Connie Lee

Born May 20, 1962

Before we talk about me, I must tell you about my parents. They are German immigrants born in 1937 and 1939 in Germany. Families being bombed, refugees walking across the country to avoid enemy armies, and always, always, not enough food were the stories I heard growing up. At age 20 and 22, my parents married and came to the United States to find a better life. They settled in New Jersey and my father became an electrician. My mother began at the lowest rung on the ladder in the field of nursing and eventually became a Registered Nurse. I have one younger brother. Very early in life, I recognized how fortunate I am in this good life and that I needed to give back to the community which has given so much to me. This was communicated to me by the life and work of my mother.

I graduated from Swarthmore College. As the child of a working class family, I was completely out of my element in this college where the other students were so much wealthier and, in all ways, so much more cosmopolitan. I took a job in a record store while going to school and felt much more comfortable with the people there. I studied psychology but knew that upon graduation I needed more experiences in "life" before continuing toward my goal of counseling. For ten years I worked as a Kelly Girl and had a great variety of jobs all the way from construction to developing software for a company. At age 30, I realized that I needed to do more with my life and so I went to graduate school for a Doctorate in Psychology. I had been living in California but managed health care made this state not a good place for employment so I went to Eastern Virginia Medical School in Norfolk, VA. where I was placed at Eastern State Hospital in Williamsburg for internship. This is where I met John, who is a psychiatrist, and who later became my husband.

I practiced psychology at the Family Living Institute and then became pregnant. It was planned for me to stay at home four to five months after the baby was born, then return to work. I quickly learned that being a psychologist doesn't necessarily prepare one for the "real thing."

John and I noticed something different about our baby daughter at two months. It was in the way she seemed to be moving. She also had colic. At four months she continued to be irritable and agitated and we knew that something wasn't right. Our pediatrician prescribed something, but within hours she was vomiting and we went to the Childrens Hospital of the King's Daughters. After an examination, the radiologist came out and said, "What I have to tell you is that your daughter's head is full of tumors." Sometimes, I think that when a parent is a health care professional, it is more difficult when things go wrong. We weren't prepared for this news. Her condition was such that she needed to have brain surgery that day or she wouldn't have lived because the tumors

134

were so large. She emerged with one leg paralyzed and she couldn't raise her head; but in three months with therapy, she was back on track. A few months later she had another bleed requiring surgery and I decided that working was just not compatible with giving our daughter my best. I also found it difficult to locate information about her condition and often times, felt quite lonely. CDR (Child Development Resources) was absolutely wonderful and I volunteered there frequently. They were my strength and support.

Soon, it became obvious that someone needed to start an association for parents and friends of someone with *cavernous angioma*, which was the diagnosis of her condition. I felt that I was in a position to contact specialists in the field as well as other parents and patients dealing with the same physical problems. Also, we were in a position to put together information as a way of connecting people. Angioma Alliance was born. My brother became involved in creating a web page, and the wheels began to move.

Now to Julia. She attends the Chesapeake Bay Academy and has adapted well to their program. At this point, she had gone through four major brain surgeries and was left with some residual affects including a mild seizure disorder and problems with attention. However, it could have been so much worse.

I had volunteered at CDR and had also been supported strongly in my role as a mother by the staff there. I really feel that I had several mentors at CDR including Cathie Allport. They, as well as my mother who is now living close enough to help, have been so good for Julia and me.

In an article in the Williamsburg Health Journal, August 2006, Page Bishop quoted me as saying, *"There's nothing about what I do that's not personal. Helping others brings a sense of fulfillment to my life, but, in the end, I know anything I do will help Julia. She is my motivation—the greatest one I could have ever imagined. Life will be better for her as a result of my actions. She will grow up in a world where there is support."*

Looking back on my life, I feel that there isn't any experience that I've had that has been wasted. So much about my life has been a synthesis of experiences and the value of what I have learned. My advice to younger women is to value the experiences of life and use them, learn from them and recognize that years later these are the things that you might put together to make a difference in your life and the lives of others. Experiences are not wasted.

Ginnie

There is a Dresden like quality to her appearance
As she sits comfortably discussing the School of Education.
Surrounded by books, framed pictures of young girls on horseback, green plants.

It could be a kitchen, a boardroom, or a classroom.
She is comfortable with the discussions, she is comfortable with herself.
A sense of homey professionalism pervades the office...and the conversation.

A beautiful smile punctuates many of her comments.
One feels the solid foundation, the wholeness of self, allowing her to blossom.
Big windows introduce the out of doors, her preference of where she likes to be.

Balance is what she advises.
Balance is what one feels.
Beauty and balance and focus in healthy combination, is Ginnie.

Virginia Laycock McLaughlin

Ginnie L. McLaughlin
Born December 15, 1949

My family lived in Baltimore, and I was the middle one of three daughters. My father was a physician, an obstetrician and gynecologist, and my mother was a full-time mother and wife. The family years were uneventful and pleasant, ones typical of the 50s. As a middle child I learned collaborative and negotiating skills which have been very useful throughout my lifetime. Relationships are extremely important and this too has shaped my professional life to a great degree.

Mom was very important in that she was a continual presence in the home. I look like my mother, have a lot of her characteristics, and admired her greatly. My father was, perhaps, even more influential in my life. Leadership skills, independent thinking and debating points (dinner table conversations were always quite lively) were the things that came from the encouragement of my father. I went to Catholic schools, and in high school, at that time, the nuns stressed achieving whatever you wanted to do and striving for your dreams. They were quite the feminists!

My definition of a "mentor" is someone who leads by example and has a personal interest in the mentee. My father was certainly a mentor to me. There have been many, many other mentors in my life, so many it's difficult to list. In terms of achievements, nothing even comes close to parenting; I have one daughter and three stepchildren.

Challenges? Well, I was adamant that I wouldn't go into education when I finished high school, mostly because it was one of the "expected choices" of a young woman at that time. Instead, I studied psychology at the College of William and Mary, but I wasn't ready to go for my PhD in that area. I was interested in special education, and it was just beginning to bloom at the time. I found I could combine both of my interests in this one area. That's how I got into the field of education.

Another one of my persistent challenges is prioritizing. I want to do everything at once. With so many competing demands, it's a constant juggling act. There is definitely a need for prioritization. However, what has worked well for me is that I have been able to seize new opportunities presented and take on new challenges. Choosing to move beyond where I was has definitely worked to my advantage. An example is, when I was 23 years old, having just completed my master's degree and teaching special education in the public schools of Charleston, South Carolina, I learned there was a part-time faculty position at The Citadel. I submitted my vitae, was accepted and taught for three years, at both undergraduate and graduate levels, where there were no women and few non-military faculty.

I then went on to get a doctoral degree, taught on the faculties at Clemson (South Carolina) and Old Dominion Universities before returning to the College of William and Mary (Virginia) as an Assistant Professor. Dean Nagle of the School of Education approached me to become Associate Dean at the age of 34. I accepted and served for seven years in that position. This is when I learned that I enjoyed academic administration. In 1992, newly appointed president Tim Sullivan asked me to be his Chief of Staff which I did for two years. Once again, this was being able to choose the unorthodox opportunity when it presented itself. After that, I came back to the faculty and was able to be a candidate for the Deanship.

I have been Dean of the William and Mary School of Education for eleven years, and can only be proud of the changes which have occurred. The School looks very different than it did ten years ago; for example, the caliber of the faculty, partnerships developed, research and grants, and private fund raising – we are in a great place. Now we are anticipating the new facility at the Sentara site (formerly the Williamsburg Sentara Hospital). This is all very thrilling.

Much of my strength comes from my faith. It has always been very much a part of me. The sense of social justice, which came both from Catholic school and my home, is ever present with me. I was married in 1972 to someone I dated all through college and began moving around following my husband's career. In the 1980s, separation, divorce and single parenting were not a part of my plan, but I was independent enough to know that I could accomplish this too if necessary. I was remarried in 1992 and we now live at "River Bend," a name chosen to reflect the twists and turns in our lives.

So often we have led our daughters to believe that they can have it all. Great struggles can be caused by this way of thinking. The attempt to balance so many needs is probably felt by most of our young women. My advice to them is to decide what really matters and to retain those priorities, even as things change. And we must be easier on ourselves. I've come to recognize and value the networks of support which I've had. Finding a nurturing support system is essential.

As far as what I plan to do next – creating the School of Education in the new facility will be the main challenge for the immediate years to come.

Viky Pedigo

The room, a library, is filled with larger than life figures,
Colors, books, stuffed animals, and art everywhere.
There are exuberant displays of books and characters.

Her woven hat sits carefully shaped and decorated at an angle on her head.
Rings flashing with expressive finger play,
Bursts of laugher punctuating phrases of serious thought.

The room and the teacher are one.
Both seem larger than life.
Color, drama, excitement… all for the love of children, teaching, and learning.

Vaudene Rose Fable Pedigo

Vaudene "Viky" Pedigo
Born December 21, 1934

I was born on the longest night of the year; the winter solstice, December 21st, in Louisville, Kentucky, right in the middle of the Great Depression – 1934. My family had moved from Indiana because my father had been employed by the Federal Land Bank. To add to the misery of the country's financial situation, along came the greatest flood in the nation's history - 1937 - when the Ohio and Mississippi Rivers overflowed their banks. My grandmother had nightmares, dreaming we were all floating away. On a more upbeat note, my first ten years were filled with the delights of Churchill Downs, even being introduced to the great triple-crown winner, Whirlaway. Other pleasant memories revolved around the Ohio River with excursions on the riverboat, the Louisville Belle.

Kindergarten for me began in January, having been born in December. Being rather social, I often ended up standing in the cloak closet (a long semi-lighted hallway between classrooms) for discipline during "rest time." I self-righteously declared to myself then and there that when I grew up, I'd be the teacher and never treat my students so unjustly. I remember my report card read, "She loves helping her classmates and continues to be quite social during quiet time."

By third grade, the family moved back to Indiana and I entered Public School #10 in Indianapolis. A very wise teacher soon realized that I needed a special "job" to best utilize my abundant energy. She placed a small desk and chair right at the back corner of the classroom where the door opened into the hallway directly across from the principal's office. When the school telephone rang, I slipped out to answer it with, "School #10, a pupil speaking." I was the school secretary.

School mid-year classes were usually small – seven to nine students – so class friendships were forged and remain constant today.

Even though my father had a white-collar job, he loved to "play the ponies" and gamble. We ate steak on payday and then cereal as the week wore on. He never met a stranger. He let my brother and me know from elementary school on that if we wanted a college education we had better do well in school and get a scholarship. So beginning at the age of nine, I always had a moneymaking job of some kind starting with a newspaper route in my neighborhood. I became very independent in time, buying what I wanted when I wanted it. My two brothers – one older and one younger – had to make their own way, too.

My younger brother was born when I was ten and a half. He became my constant companion, and even though he now lives in California, we keep in close touch. His email to me on my last birthday was addressed: "to my favorite person in the world."

In my early teens my parents were divorced and my mother resumed working as a PBX Operator for the New York Central System. My mother was always the responsible one and I believe I share characteristics of both parents. She and I shared the care of my younger brother and when he started school, I went back with him to my alma mater, School #10. This time, I was the paid part-time secretary, working afternoons during my sophomore year at Arsenal Technical High School. This outstanding school is a former World War I army arsenal with a huge campus and a rigorous academic program. In the evenings, I attended my brother's conferences and even the PTA meetings. Frequently, when a teacher had to leave her class to attend a meeting, I was allowed to "substitute" in grades K-8.

During my senior year, I was back in an elementary school, this time in a pilot program called "cadet teaching." Two of us students actually went out and worked in classrooms much the same as student teachers in college do today. I graduated seventh out of a class of a thousand students and was offered scholarships to several Indiana Universities. I accepted a full scholarship to Butler University in Indianapolis because I could live at home and keep my position as a touring agent for the Shell Oil Company. I was active in the Butler Independents' Student Organization, even eking out time to be Sophomore Cotillion Queen and a member of the homecoming court.

As a youth leader in the Presbyterian Church, I was also honored with a six-week summer scholarship sponsored by the International Order of the King's Daughters and Sons to Chautauqua, New York, before I began college. I was the "Indiana girl" among the students from all fifty states and several foreign countries. This was the seat of my awakening to grand opera, New York Theater, and symphonic music. We scholarship students dressed formally and ushered at all of the special performances. It truly was "a little bit of heaven on earth."

A seven-month whirlwind romance culminated in marriage in the middle of final exams during my senior year. You see, in those days, it was unheard of for a couple to cohabit unless they were married. It was time for me to establish my independence anyway, so we found a lovely apartment. To make expenses we shared our new place with a wonderful friend in a "three's company" arrangement. Since it was a one-bedroom, our friend had a "pull-out-of-the-wall" Murphy bed in the living room. I remember living on bananas, cereal, and pasta.

After teaching one year in Indianapolis, graduate school at Emory University in Atlanta beckoned. Tired of the miserable cold winters in the Midwest we sought out the warm welcome arms of the south. My husband earned both Master's and Doctorate degrees while I taught seventh grade for three years and received my Master's degree. My first seventh grade class had an enrollment of 48 students. The school was new, the library was empty, so where else could you put us? We had no special area for teachers or planning periods. We taught all day with no breaks – even eating with our students. Thank goodness I was young and energetic. Elementary school culminated with seventh grade so we were the big kids working as the safety patrol. The Atlanta Police Department sponsored a whole train for her loyal safety patrol guards to spend a week in Washington, D.C. We marched down Constitution Avenue and took in all the sites of the city. We also performed in the Robert Chandler Harris's Folk Dance Festival, had formal school dances, and took top prizes in the local Science Fair. I also introduced the new fifth-grade science curriculum on statewide television.

My touring service experience helped us decide where to continue our teaching careers. I had traveled vicariously to Williamsburg on many occasions, so we decided our first choice would be the College of William and Mary and Williamsburg/James City County Public Schools. One of my mentors was my principal in Atlanta who gave me a glowing recommendation, paving the way for me to have long phone conversations with the WJCC superintendent, Rawls Byrd. In 1960, Rawls Byrd and his secretary, Lucille Garrison, were the entire central office staff. I taught second and third grades at Matthew Whaley Elementary. During weekends and summers, I worked as a hostess for Colonial Williamsburg under the direction of Elizabeth Callis and Shirley Lowe.

Jeanne Etheridge was my principal, and when I became pregnant, I felt obligated to tell her (in those days you rarely continued in the classroom past three months or when you began to "show"). It was spring break, and she asked, "Where is it dahling, and are you sure?" I am not sure that she was convinced, and since I had made all these beautiful clothes designed to disguise my condition, I continued teaching until the end of the school year. One week later, we welcomed Lance Allen who became, and still is, the center of my life. Born on the night of July 3rd, he just missed my older brother's birthday, July 4th.

My younger brother had given me a lot of childcare experience, but this boy was all consuming. I knew I wanted to stay home with him during his early years. This was a squeeze financially, and my husband found it difficult to accept that he was the #2 man in the household. After four years, he accepted another position elsewhere, and I began life as a single parent. I did have to go back to work, but I could take my son with me to Greenwood Nursery and Kindergarten.

To re-enter the public school system, I taught Head Start which led to a first grade position at Rawls Byrd School. Lance was always able to be with me when I was in school – one way or another. Another mentor was Rawls Byrd's Principal, Theresa Runyans. She studied the ungraded British Primary System in England. When she returned to the States, she saw that Rawls Byrd School, with its pod system of buildings, was ideally suited to develop the primary – grade program. Each family of grades 1-3 had four teachers, two teaching assistants, and about 100 students. One of the teachers was designated as team leader – in actuality, a mini-principal – and this became my responsibility. In 1974 I developed nodes on my vocal chords, and was advised to find another vocation; but how could I leave this profession I loved? Why not combine my love of teaching with my love of beautiful books – and move into the library!

Libraries are quiet places, aren't they? Library science certification was gained through courses held all over the peninsula. Theresa Runyans approved my decision since she always said, "the library is the heart of the school," and she had been a librarian herself.

Once my son was safely ensconced in James Madison University, I expanded my teaching by first establishing myself as the regular high school library/media specialist for the summer school program. I taught Children's Literature as an adjunct professor at the College of William and Mary for three years. I really enjoyed expanding my fellow teachers' love of literature for young children and then watching them use their knowledge to enhance the curriculum. Eventually, I began teaching adult education classes two to four nights a week. I worked with adults just learning to read, all the way up to those seeking the GED. I often worked with the parents of the students that I taught during the day.

Teaching had allowed me to choose a flexible working schedule that has provided me the opportunity to travel to such amazing places as the rain forests of Costa Rica, the wild animal parks of Africa, and the exotic Galapagos Islands.

Williamsburg has been a nurturing environment for both my son and me. The college, the community, and Colonial Williamsburg have been our treasure and our pleasure.

My advice to young women is to simply build close ties with family and friends and find something you love to do. If you hear the music of a different drummer, follow it; and if you want something bad enough, you will find a way to do it.

Ethel's Story

Is it her graceful, beautifully manicured hands?
Could it be the dramatic shock of white hair that dips onto her forehead?
Is it her compact figure, held in perfect posture sitting or standing?
Perhaps it is the remnants of her native tongue in the German accent.
The physical aspects are a small part of her beauty.
"I don't hate anyone" comes from one who experienced WW II
and the darkest side of life.
Fatherless early, widowed for 25 years; she still smiles warmly,
casting light as she talks.
Her strength is from within and it seems to grow as she shares it with others.
Her love of life itself is worn like a cloak about her shoulders.
Her gift to all of us is her presence and her story.

Ethel Adolf Sternberg

Ethel Adolf Sternberg
Born September 3, 1924

I was born in Hamburg, Germany. My father was born in Austria and immigrated to Germany as did my mother from Poland and both were of the Jewish faith. My parents owned a wholesale grocery business that was quite successful because of its location in a prosperous, gentile neighborhood. My father fought for Germany in World War I. Later he became sick from an injury in the brain caused by a bullet and he died eight years later. After my father's death, my mother took over the business.

My mother was my mentor. She taught me everything: scrubbing floors, knitting, sewing and doing all the things to run a home. More than that, she prepared me for the intangible things I needed to deal with in life.

My parents thought it was important that Kurt, my older brother by two years and only sibling, and I be taught in the Jewish faith. We attended a Jewish school, located in a Jewish neighborhood, about half an hour away from where we lived. All our friends and playmates, however, were the gentile children in our neighborhood.

During my early childhood, my life was quite normal. Germany was experiencing the Depression, but my parents' business was not affected too much. They continued to do well. But, when things began to happen to the Jews, my mother, who now ran the business by herself, started sending money to her two brothers in New York. They could use it for our education if my brother and I had to go to America. Although, my mother never believed that anything would happen to any of us because of my father's patriotism in giving his life for "the Fatherland."

By 1938, things changed. My brother and I began to experience social isolation as our gentile friends were not allowed to speak to us. My mother's business was getting bad because her former customers were not allowed to do business with Jews. Then came "Krystallnacht." The only thing I remember about that was someone wrote "Jew" on our front window. My mother just washed it off. The next day on our way to school, we saw all the destruction in the city from the rampage the night before. The fires were still burning and covering the streets was glass crushed from broken windows. It was horrible. Then, one week later, three very large SS soldiers came to our store (we were living in an apartment behind) and said "out!" We were allowed to take a few possessions with us. We were given a beautiful apartment of eight rooms but, within weeks, we had six more people added to the household. We didn't have problems with food because my mother had connections in the "black market." She could see things changing quickly and got us passports to leave Germany. Mine had a "J" on it and bore the name Ethel Sara Adolf. ("Sara" was added to all female Jewish passports, so that it was immediately recognized that I was a Jew, and "Israel" was added to my brother's.)

Mother sent us to Spain with a group of about twenty people locked in a train car. When we got off in Barcelona, we found that the boat tickets for America, which my mother paid for in Germany, were no good. So mother sent money to my uncles in America to send money through an aid organization. This paid for us to live in a small hotel in Spain. We were required to check in at the police station every day. My brother and I became friendly with the hotel owners and one day they were warned by a friend not to allow the children to go to the station that day. I pretended that I was sick, moaning in bed and saying that I needed my brother to stay with me. A Spanish doctor was called and he wrote a note saying that I must remain in bed for the day. The others in the group did go to the station and were taken across the Pyrenees into occupied France where they were sent on to concentration camps. The hotel family continued to take care of us, even wanting to adopt us if we would become Roman Catholic.

By this time, I was 15 and my mother was still in Hamburg. She wrote letters to us. While most of the Jews who could had left, my mother was unable to get out. Her Polish birth and the strict quota system prevented it. The last letter from her begged her brothers in America to get her out. She said that if she could not, she would be going to a place where no bombs fell, a beautiful place where her father was. (He was dead.) My brother kept this letter a secret and protected me from the truth about what happened to our mother.

Eventually, we were assisted by the Hebrew Association Aiding Immigrants (HAIS), which sent us to Philadelphia and then on to New York to meet the uncles. They were older, had a small apartment on Delaney Street and were not used to having children around (I was 15 years old and Kurt was 17). So after a few nights of cramped living, we went back to the HAIS asking them to please take us back. We both went out and got jobs. When we had accumulated $74, we found an apartment and began a new independent life. Six months later, Kurt was inducted into the Navy so I got another woman to share the apartment and we stayed there two years. My brother was stationed at Camp Peary, Virginia. On a leave he met a nice family from Richmond who invited him and me, as well, to visit. Eventually, we both moved to Richmond. Kurt started a business, Adolf's Jewelry Store, which, since his death, has been run by his two sons.

I met my husband in Richmond and we lived there until 1950 when we came to Williamsburg. At that time, there was only one other Jewish family here. We decided that we wanted to give our children a religious foundation and education so that when they became adults, they would have a faith. They could chose another, but, of course, we hoped that they remained Jewish. So we started a temple, Temple Beth El. My husband was president for 15 years and my whole life was the temple. We met in homes, the Wren Chapel, wherever we could until my husband found the piece of property on Jamestown Rd. Then we bought a house from Colonial Williamsburg and moved it to that lot. By then there were about 18 Jewish families and everybody worked together.

My husband became ill and I cared for him for ten years. I did a lot of needlepoint and cross-stitch handwork while he was dying. It was during this time that I lost my religious faith. Some time after he died, I began to see that this way of thinking was dumb! I returned to the temple and was its president for nine years. In 1996 we rebuilt the inside. I feel a real sense of accomplishment about Temple Beth El, which means "House of God."

My brother had protected me from the truth about my mother from the time we left Germany and went to Spain. I didn't know until about ten years ago when he read my mother's letters to me. The last letter in which she begged for help getting out of Germany and foretold her own death was heartbreaking. I got a book from Germany where it listed all the Jews from Hamburg who were killed and there was her name on the first page. She was gassed the first day at the Litzmannstadt Concentration Camp in Poland. I was totally numb.

I decided then that I needed to go out and talk: to school children, college students, and any groups who were interested in my story. This has been a good experience for me.

From a letter by teachers at Toano Middle School (Mr. Brown, Mrs. Woolwine, Mrs. Andre) *"Thank you again for visiting the Waves team here at Toano Middle School. As you can see, you had a huge impact on our students. The hour you spent in our presence instilled in us a lifetime of understanding. It is a wonderful lesson for the kids to see that your struggles in life have made you even stronger. You are strength in its purest form. To us, you are invincible. We are so blessed that you were able to share your story with us. My young men felt like princes when they recognized that they were escorting a Queen. My young ladies stared in adoration realizing that you are what they are striving to become. Thank you for adding 'A Touch of Class' to Toano Middle School."*

I have recorded for the Spielberg Foundation SHOAH . I am also included in the book TO LIFE, STORIES OF COURAGE AND SURVIVAL told by Hampton Roads Holocaust survivors, liberators and rescuers and in the movie, *To Bear Witness.*

My advice to young women is that you must be prepared to live independently, to take care of yourself, and to have basic life skills. Family is so important and friends are as well. Every day I get up I have a purpose, something which I expect to accomplish during the day. I exercise every day, work with my hands and keep my mind busy reading or doing crossword puzzles. I work three days a week at a local jewelry store and do things with my friends and travel when I can.

As for my faith, I participate in temple activities but I can also pray to God at home. I consider my three children as my greatest accomplishment and now have six grandchildren as well. They have written to me about their memories of religious holidays, what we ate and what I said in our home…for the last 50 years. This is beautiful for me and shows what is most important in my life.

(l-r) Liz Montgomery, Ever Dorsey, Ethell B. Hill, Margaret Stockton, Myrtle Engs, Catherine Parker and Earleen Robinson (Patricia Wells not pictured)

Le Cercle Charmant

Le Cercle Charmant's History

Le Cercle Charmant was organized in October 1944, by a group of young African American women who were educators at Bruton Heights School. The club started out as a social and educational origination. The first name of the club was "The Charming Circle" as suggested by the club's founder and first president, Esther P. Hill. After that, Zelda Gray suggested that the name should be translated into French to give the club a more special identification. They supported offering scholarships to deserving area students and organizing, sponsoring and promoting social activities in the community. Other founding members included: Olive Daughtry, Zelda Gray, Rosalie Jones Griffin, Marion Johnson, Carletha Ransome Palmer, Edna Parker, Elizabeth Meade Proctor and Hattie J. Sasser.

Minnie Robinson, Bobbye Alexander, Dorothy Purnell, Jean Fenton, Opelene L. Davis, Ann Brown and Jacquelyn R. Gardner

Oral tradition tells the story of a small group of women educators at Bruton Heights School during the 1940s when Bruton Heights School replaced the aging James City County Training School (grades 1–11). Bruton Heights was built as a "model school" with the assistance of John D. Rockefeller, Jr. It is told that in the late 1930s a group of parents, business people and clergy members formed The Negro School League. They wrote a strongly worded letter to the Colonial Williamsburg Foundation and the Williamsburg School Board asking what could be done for their community in that many of the Negro properties were being bought for the restoration. The result was that families and businesses were being displaced. Of particular concern was the need for a new school for African American students to replace the outdated and overcrowded agricultural training school. The plan for Bruton Heights School grew out of the League's efforts. Rockefeller gave the land (about 30 acres) for the school and his wife, Abby Aldrich Rockefeller, contributed $50,000 of her own money. Others in the community contributed funds, and there was a $50,000 local bond issue. The federal Works Progress Administration appropriated over $90,000 for the project. The local school board operated Bruton Heights School.

In the summer of 1940 before Bruton Heights was to open in September, Rockefeller contacted a Columbia University professor and friend to come to Williamsburg to conduct workshops for teachers at the newly completed school. Teachers were recruited from Hampton University, Norfolk State College and from further away. Retired Bruton Heights teacher Madeline Gee once told the story of "camping out" in the school cafeteria because there was no housing available for Negro teachers coming into the town. This expanding group of educated women lacked many avenues for either social or cultural activity outside of the school, so they began to meet in homes to discuss how they could continue the efforts of raising standards and opportunities for their students as well as to support one another. Thus was the beginning of the organization, Le Cercle Charmant, whose motto is "Serving with Charm and Dignity."

In 1946 the Club increased its membership and accepted Clemenza Braxton and Celeste Dobson into the Club. New members were added over the years. In 1948 the club sponsored its first "Miss Queen of Charm Pageant" as a fund-raiser for that year. Under the leadership of president Ruth Pope, regular monthly business meetings were established on the second Tuesday from September to June. This practice continues today with the club members hosting the meetings. The Charm Pageant was discontinued, then reinstated in 1977 and was an annual event until 1994. For seventeen years, this pageant culminated in one young woman crowned "the Queen of Charm"; however, for 10 months preceding the big formal event, there was mentoring by Le Cercle members for each one of the girls entering the contest. This included such things as the etiquette of how to conduct oneself properly in various social situations and other social graces so that they would be better prepared later in life. The competition required each entrant to demonstrate talent and poise.

Le Cercle Charmant began to change its focus and projects as circumstances changed in the community. While many social activities for the membership consumed much of their time and resources, members decided to provide more community outreach services as well. The focus has continued to be the needs of the people and the community. Currently, scholarships for students in each high school are awarded annually. The members have become involved in efforts including Breast Cancer Awareness, AIDS Network, Avalon, Housing Partnerships, Fish and the Community Action agency. They have also become personally involved in many local organizations by holding board memberships. The club is proud of its continued annual commitment and support of the NAACP, Black History Programs, an Evening of Elegance and scholarship awards.

There are 15 members. Interestingly, a majority of them are retired teachers. Each one of the women has an important story. This is indeed a group of Remarkable Women making a difference in the community and beyond.

Bobbye B. Alexander

Obstacles to overcome included the fact that Negroes (as we were known then) had to leave the state of Florida to get higher education. I studied in New York for math education. The important mentors in my life were my parents and Dr. Mary McCloud Bethune, advisor to presidents. Having been raised and surrounded by God-fearing people, I could only succeed. One of my efforts in the community is the ACT-SO (Afro-Academic, Technological, and Scientific Olympics) program in which I've been involved for 20 years. This is one of the NAACP's efforts to harness the talent of African American high school students. As a national program, winners in our area compete with students from throughout the United States. Colonial Williamsburg Foundation supports the Martin Luther King/NAACP/ACT-SO community breakfast so that all the funds go toward student housing and travel for the competition. I was one of the founders of the League of Women Voters and the Williamsburg AIDS Network. My first love, though, is work in the Baptist Church and community service. Advice I might give to young women is to have God in their lives, to use all of the gifts given by God and I do believe that the greatest gift is love.

Bobbye holds the longest membership (over 50 years) in Le Cercle Charmant.

Ann Brown

Getting a college degree was my dream. There were many obstacles in that I took care of my husband and three children, my mother who lived with us, and I worked a full-time job along with going to school. I could not have accomplished this without the full support of my family. By having both a bachelor and master's degree it was possible to work as a counselor, social worker and elementary teacher. I was appointed to the Election Board for James City County in 2001. One year later, I was elected to the JCC School Board and became the Chair in 2005. The Governor appointed me to the Commonwealth Council on Aging for a four-year term. Even though I started rather late, I would advise young women to set goals for yourself and never give up on being successful.

Opelene L. Davis

With guidance from my parents, the teachers, and the church, I managed to go beyond the expectations of the time in that there was segregation and few opportunities for advancement. Since my mother was an educator, she was a very important figure in my life and motivation to achieve. My accomplishments include being a representative for the state with employment and training of persons seeking jobs, seeking new employers for the area and setting up programs for youth. I've also been a role model to two sons and two nieces who I also raised and they are all educated and successful in life. To all young people I would say to get a good education and have high moral standards.

Ever L Dorsey

An obstacle I had to overcome was a basic shyness and trying to be true to myself. My mother, teachers, friends and husband have all been important in helping me to have faith in myself. Travel and living in other countries, marriage and the loss of loved ones have all been significant turning points in my life. My husband was a career officer and we were part of the occupation force in Japan after the war. This was an amazing experience for young people who had never been far from home. We also lived in France, where I learned the language by living with an adopted family for a year. We are still in touch with people from that assignment. Nieces and nephews, "adopted" children from all over the world have so enriched my life. It is important to learn to concentrate on what is worthwhile in life. My advice to young women is be true to yourself and "Go, girl, go!"

Myrtle C. Engs

Growing up during the Great Depression, we had little income and no savings. It was the determination of my family, especially my mother, and teachers who encouraged me to further education. Marriage to an Army officer enabled me to travel to 11 foreign countries. Life opportunities included raising three wonderful, successful children and teaching so many precious children. Contributing to the community, I served as a Trustee of Thomas Nelson Community College, Regional Library Board Member and the vestry of St. Martin's Episcopal church. God has blessed me with the ability, motivation and resources to accomplish what I have. I would say to young women, get a thorough education, always strive to do your best in every facet of your life, trust in the Lord and most of all, "love your neighbor."

Jean M. Fenton

A major obstacle to me was growing up in the segregated south with limited access to the educational and culturally enriching experiences that were available in Norfolk. Even though my father did not have extensive formal education, he always had the vision that I should get a doctorate. A choice that helped me succeed was to become a teacher at the Virginia Commonwealth University and to pursue a doctorate. My teachers had such high hopes and high expectations for me.

As the first African American woman with an Ed.D. in the Newport News School Division in which I worked, and first to be appointed Assistant Superintendent, I served as a role model and mentor for many African Americans and women. To young women I would say dare to be yourself. Don't depend upon the reflection of yourself in the eyes of others to dictate who you are or what you are worth.

Jacquelyn R. Gardner

My parents kept us involved in community activities such as Brownies, Girl Scouts, Sunday school and always expected us to do well. I imitated my schoolteachers at Bruton

Heights which contributed to my having high expectations of myself. I enrolled in the graduate program at Hampton University and for 36 years as a teacher and administrator in education, I tried to live and work by their standards of excellence, their preparation of promising students for positions of leadership and service. I was president of the Virginia Head Start Directors, appointed by Governor Douglass Wilder to serve on the Virginia Council on Child Day Care and Early Childhood Programs and served on various committees. Hopefully, I made a positive impact on the lives of hundreds of children and families in the community. Raising and educating our two children, who are doing well in their chosen careers, is also an accomplishment. Young women need to hear that they can do anything they put their heart into and imagine their achievements.

Jackie is the only member native to Williamsburg.

Ethell B. Hill

One of the obstacles I encountered growing up in a small country town was not being prepared for college when I entered. When I was growing up, I was told that if I wanted to get ahead I had to go to school and use my head. I was told that as a black person in a white society that no one was going to help me so I had better be prepared to work hard. I was also told that "no matter how good I was" that it was not going to be good enough—so develop a thick skin and keep on going

My family kept me on track…my aunt Grace mainly; also my aunt Alma and my grandmother. They were the mainstay. I was determined to let my family know that I could do just fine. I completed a master's program …and found that everything I had been told was true but that I was prepared.

Advising young women, I would say go to school and learn and get educated. Before you try to take care of someone else, take care of yourself. Have confidence and a belief in yourself and God, and that you are capable of many things.

Liz Montgomery

Obstacles? Yes! Financial resources were limited yet we had everything we needed. Eight other brothers and sisters shared what we had. My mother and father gave me everything I needed to live and survive. But I remember the 60s, at age 19, sitting at a lunch counter being unable to use a restroom marked "white only" when I couldn't wait, and I had to go outside around the corner, in the dark on dirt floor…that was my challenge. Today the challenge is technology. I was fortunate, for I lived for music and my passion to sing. I chose to be a single parent when it was not "popular." What would I say to young women? The sky is the limit. Education is the key. Be true to your passion whatever it is and develop that passion with all your might. My concern is that today, the village/community is not as involved in the total welfare of the child as when I grew up. It was The Village that helped me become what I am today. My faith, my family and music have enriched my life and made me a very fulfilled person!

Catherine Parker

As an adult I have overcome many obstacles and the most glaring ones were work related. In my forties, I embarked on a career in telecommunications which required me to pass a series of complex exams. With substantial coaching and mentoring from two colleagues, I was able to pass the exam and eventually pass a more difficult exam which was required for the next position level. I regarded this as a significant accomplishment. As a child growing up in North Carolina we were blessed to have two strong parents who taught us that we were African Princesses with a proud family heritage. As a result all my siblings grew up with considerable personal esteem and confidence. This was tremendously helpful as I moved to New York, started a family and began my career. My advice to young women is to believe in themselves and treasure their rich history and heritage.

Dorothy C. Purnell

The greatest obstacles I've had to overcome were medical problems. During the time I was bedridden in childhood due to rheumatic fever, I had a visiting teacher. This was during 4th through 7th grades. Even though the doctor had predicted an early death, this teacher encouraged me not to give up. Finally, I was able to complete additional education and then attended community college. My husband and I operated a travel agency for years and this provided us with the opportunity to travel to many parts of the world. In addition to early medical problems, I am a breast cancer survivor, twice.

I'm proud of what we have accomplished and thankful to God for all. My thoughts for young women are to set goals, stay focused, get the necessary education, be self-sufficient and have the confidence necessary to succeed in whatever is attempted.

B. Earleen Robinson

The obstacle to accomplish my goal was limited finances - so I worked a year before entering college. Being the only black person in most of my high school and college classes, I persevered in maintaining a high academic record. My parents had a very important influence upon me in educational and other of my life's endeavors. My career led to the position of administrator of an elementary school with more than 800 students and five special education classes and I also led a city-wide Parental Involvement Program. What I would say to young women is to pursue their dreams and anticipate setbacks but not to allow them to alter your plans. The multiplicity of choices young women have today might be an asset to some but creates a dilemma for others.

Minnie Robinson

Encouragement from parents, other family members and teachers were what made it possible to gain meaningful employment. As I left North Carolina and lived in New York and New Jersey, more opportunities became available. My work for the Sony Corporation in customer services eventually allowed me to retire. I plan to continue in my service to community and to my church.

Speaking to our young women, I see the multiplicity of choices facing them as a possible problem and yet it also provides more choices for job opportunities. Getting a good education is absolutely necessary.

Margaret Carrington Stockton

Obstacles such as jealousy, a bit of prejudice and finances I met with perseverance and a commitment to finish whatever I start. Excellent teachers and role models, strong faith and family support made the difference for me. It was difficult to manage financing as well as to gain admission to Harvard University. My educational achievements allowed me to pursue a profession that touches many lives and I have had the privilege of teaching in New York, Michigan and Virginia. In many instances this was the first time these kids had had an African American teacher. I felt it was an accomplishment when selected to teach a mandated human relations course through the University of Virginia to administrators, teachers, and school board members. Travel and having a wide variety of diverse individuals in my life have allowed me to grow as an individual. Young women will need to learn from other cultures, travel, be open minded and open to new experiences, learn to manage money and be better prepared educationally than their colleagues in order to be competitive. The changes in our values and expectations allow women now to be competing for top-level jobs.

Patricia McGough Wells

My mother, who had seven children and very little money, managed very well. She told us that we were as good as the next and it didn't matter that we were "Negroes." She talked constantly about the necessity of a good education. I grew up in Texas where the schools were segregated and there was plenty of racism; but graduating from college and getting out of a bad marriage were very significant turning points in my life. I impressed upon my two children the need for education and one is a medical doctor, the other a registered nurse. What I would say to young women is to be strong, have high standards and know that there are consequences for actions. Don't settle for less and make good choices!

2003 Edition

Big Hugs To:

Donald Brady, our technician, courier and unfailing encourager
Ron Lenthall, our editorial advisor, sounding board and supporter
Karin Clamann, our layout designer and Pagemaker expert
Joan Swanson and Joann Meeks, our proofreaders and friends

Many Thanks To:

Mr. Bill Cozens, David Banks, and Carolee Owens at AlphaGraphics

Anne Conkling, Dr. Kate Slevin, Sociology Department at the College of William and Mary, Jerry at Aromas, Jim Sheahan, Suzie Dell, Allison Lenthall, Bill Crawford, Dennis Montgomery, Kirk Mariner, Will Molineaux, Jeanne Zeidler, Bettina Manzo at the Swem Library, Sarah's Group, Birmingham (MI) Area Senior Citizen Center (BASCC), Paul Aron, Libbey Oliver, Bob Pruitt, David Tetrault, Sandy Swift, Carol Weaver, Janet Lenthall, Bill Doig

2007 Edition

More Hugs and Thanks To:

Joan Swanson, Sheila Zubkoff, Linda H. Rowe (Historian for The Colonial Williamsburg Foundation), Hal Geisking, Carol Weaver (Bruton Parish Book and Gift Shop), Jim Joseph, Pat Hernlund, Professor Emeritus, Wayne State University

Photo Credits

Donald Brady, Page 118
Cary Oliva, Pages 10, 14, 18, 22, 27, 32, 36, 40, 45, 50, 54, 59, 64, 67, 71, 75, 82, 86, 90, 95, 99, 103, 108
Dr. Ellen Rudolph, Pages 112, 124, 128, 133, 137, 141, 147, 152, 153